Walks in Edinburgh's Old Town

The Authors

Michael and Elspeth Wills first came to know the Old Town when they moved to the Grassmarket over twenty years ago. At the time they wanted to settle in the country. Without a car, however, they opted to live in the heart of the city instead, a decision which they have never regretted. Involvement in local activities made them realise what a vibrant, varied and enduring community they had joined. Curiosity led them to explore what lay behind the familiar frontages of the Royal Mile. This book is the result of their journey into the Old Town, past and present.

Michael and Elspeth are also the authors of *Walks in Edinburgh's New Town*.

WALKS IN EDINBURGH'S OLD TOWN

Michael and Elspeth Wills

THE MERCAT PRESS

First published in 1997 by Mercat Press
James Thin, 53 South Bridge, Edinburgh EH1 1YS
This revised edition published 2001

ISBN 1873644 698

To Betty,
and all good neighbours
in the Old Town

Set in Omega at Mercat Press
Printed and bound in Great Britain by
Bell & Bain Ltd, Glasgow

CONTENTS

List of maps
vii

Introduction
1

The Development of the Old Town
10

Walk 1: Soldiers, Ministers and Prime Ministers
The Castle Esplanade to Bank Street
24

Walk 2: Advocates, Councillors and Journalists
Bank Street to North Bridge
34

Walk 3: Bishops, Reformers and Survivors
North Bridge to Jeffrey Street
44

Walk 4: Moors, Poets and Palfreys
Jeffrey Street to Holyrood
52

Walk 5: Brewers, Teachers and Knights
Holyrood to St Mary's Street
61

Walk 6: Robbers, Skinners and Paupers
St Mary's Street to South Bridge
70
Walk 7: Judges, Prisoners and Reformers
South Bridge to George IV Bridge
78
Walk 8: Burgher, Mason and Burglar
George IV Bridge to the Castle
84
Walk 9: Surgeons, Students and Physicians
The University Quarter
92
Walk 10: Maggie Dickson, Greyfriars Bobby
and Jingling Geordie
The Old Town South of the Castle
100

LIST OF MAPS

Edinburgh's Old Town 9
The Castle Esplanade to Bank Street 25
Bank Street to North Bridge 33
North Bridge to Jeffrey Street 43
Jeffrey Street to Holyrood 51
Holyrood to St Mary's Street 62
St Mary's Street to South Bridge 71
South Bridge to George IV Bridge 77
George IV Bridge to the Castle 85
The University Quarter 91
The Old Town South of the Castle 101

INTRODUCTION

This guide describes ten walks exploring the closes of the Old Town of Edinburgh. They will take you away from the traffic and crowds into parts of the Old Town that most visitors do not discover. Each walk takes about half an hour and lets you see another side of the historic city. Yet you will never be far from a pub or cafe, and all the major sights and museums of the Old Town are on your route.

This second edition has been fully revised to take account of the many changes, large and small, that have taken place in the Old Town since the first edition was published in 1997. Most notable is the redevelopment of the site of the former brewery at the foot of the Canongate. The filling in of the area between the Canongate and Holyrood Road in the traditional pattern complete with several new closes, a spectacular Millennium visitor attraction and the headquarters of the *Scotsman* newspaper, significant in themselves, were eclipsed by the choice of the site opposite Holyrood Palace for the new Scottish Parliament building. Walk 5 has been rerouted to take in these exciting developments.

This is not a guide to the major sights of the Old Town.

There are many such guides available. It aims instead to lead you to some of the lesser-known corners, and point out what can be seen along the way.

Many of the closes contain attractive corners, picturesque features and surprising views. Some are remarkably green and pleasant places in which to stroll or sit. One or two are rather gloomy or, on occasion, downright grubby. They are all, however, part of Edinburgh's long and romantic history and have their own character and atmosphere.

In order to put the walks in context the next chapter gives a brief outline of the history and development of the Old Town over the centuries. The emphasis is on the lives of those who lived and still live here rather than on the national events for which the Old Town was often the stage.

The Closes

Before the end of the eighteenth century there were no roads running off the Royal Mile above the Netherbow Port except the steep and narrow West Bow, winding up from the Grassmarket. Five- and six-storey tenements, known as 'lands', formed a continuous wall from one end of the street to the other. Between the lands lay narrow closes, running down the sides of the ridge and giving access to the properties behind. It was in these closes and courts that the life of the Old Town took place, and to some extent still does.

The Language of the Closes

'Close' is the term most commonly used in Edinburgh for a narrow passage between houses. Other terms you will encounter on the walks are

Court: an open area surrounded by buildings
Entry : a way into a court or close
Pend: an entry or close which passes under a building
Wynd : a slightly wider passage capable of admitting a small cart

The use of these terms, however, is not consistent and seems to be determined largely by historical accident.

Other terms used in describing the walks are:

Mouth: The opening of a close, entry or pend onto the street
Head: The higher end of a close
Foot: The lower end of a close

The closes are generally named after someone more or less famous who at one time lived or owned property there. Historically the names have changed as residents came and went. Whose name 'stuck', to become the modern 'official' name seems almost to be a matter of chance. A few are named after the markets or offices to which they led. Inevitably the spelling of the

Riddle's Close

3

close names has also varied over time, and in some cases remains uncertain. We have tried to follow that used on modern signs.

In the eighteenth century there were well over a hundred closes. Many have been destroyed in the process of providing road access to the Old Town, of slum clearance or of comprehensive redevelopment. Others have been incorporated into private property and are permanently locked.

How many closes, courts, entries and pends still remain is a matter of definition. A recent count identified 83 off the Royal Mile, but included permanently gated closes and dummy ones within the Crowne Plaza Hotel. Since then, at least three more closes have been reconstructed and one, formerly closed, restored and opened.

Followed in full, the walks will take you into over 60 closes, courts, pends or entries off the Royal Mile and a further 9 on the walks beyond. Most are named in gold lettering on black cast-iron plates. Where a street repaving scheme has been completed, the name can also be found in raised letters in the paving at the close mouth. Many have plaques just inside the close mouth giving information about notable people or events associated with the close. Some figures are well known; others require an extensive knowledge of Scottish history and literature to appreciate! The plaques are a useful supplement to the information in this guide.

The Walks

Walks 1 to 4 take you down the north side of the Royal Mile from the Castle to Holyrood Palace. Walks 5 to 8 return from Holyrood to the Castle by the south side. Walks 9 and 10 extend a little away from the Royal Mile itself. Walk 9 takes you into the University quarter, associated with Edinburgh's traditional pre-eminence in education and particularly medicine, while Walk 10 covers the Grassmarket area—and Greyfriars Bobby.

Each walk starts and finishes at an easily found point on the Royal Mile: at the Castle, George IV Bridge, the Bridges, St Mary's Street / Jeffrey Street or Holyrood. Sketch maps show the route of each walk to help you find your way. The Old Town map shows all the walks and how they relate to each other.

As the closes run down the sides of the ridge on which the Old Town is set, the walks inevitably involve some climbing and quite a lot of steps. Walks 2, 3 and 7 are particularly energetic, while Walks 1, 4 and 5 are relatively level. The summary at the start of each walk gives an indication of the demands it makes. If the climbing gets too much, the maps indicate some obvious short-cuts.

The walks provide you with routes past or very near to the many sights of the Old Town, ranging from St Giles to the Scotch Whisky Heritage Centre, from Holyrood Palace to the Museum of Childhood and Dynamic Earth.

Each walk is estimated to take approximately half an hour or, for Walks 9 and 10, a little longer. Of course it is possible to cover the ground in a lot less time, or to linger longer. All the walks could be accomplished in one, pretty energetic, day!

Each walk is designed to be complete in itself and they can be done in any order. With the aid of the maps you can even do any given walk backwards. Since all the first eight walks return to the Royal Mile at very regular intervals you are unlikely to get lost! The Old Town Map allows you to pick your own route.

Practicalities

These are urban walks and nothing more than normal city clothing and comfortable footwear is required. That said, it is possible to find the odd bit of mud in the closes in wet weather. Another hazard is the green algae, the scourge of Edinburgh stonework. You will see it in many of the closes, coating the stone in a not particularly attractive colour. No cure has yet been found short of washing it off with disinfectant, and on the paving it can be slippery when wet.

The Old Town continues to change and develop. Buildings are repaired and find new uses. Closes may be blocked off, permanently or temporarily, while others may after many years be opened up. While every attempt has been made to ensure that the information given is correct at the time of going to press, there will inevitably be further changes, both temporary and permanent. The maps suggest routes to bypass any obstacles.

Most closes are public rights of way and are open at all

Hyndford's Close

times. A few, for example Trunk's Close, Baron Maule's Close, Old Playhouse Close and the entrances to Old College and the Old Infirmary, may be locked outside working hours; if possible, try to do Walks 3, 5 and 9 on a weekday. Again, the maps will enable you to find a way round to continue the route.

There are public conveniences in Castle Wynd North just outside the Castle Esplanade and at Hunter's Square on the Bridges. Refreshments are available in a wide range of pubs, cafes and tearooms throughout the walks.

LRT's number 35 bus runs up and down the Royal Mile from Holyrood to the Lawnmarket, providing a way of getting back to your starting point. Open-topped tourist buses also run along the Royal Mile. While considerably more expensive than the service buses, a ticket on these allows you to get on and off anywhere throughout a day and includes a conducted tour of the rest of the city.

Enjoy your walk!

west

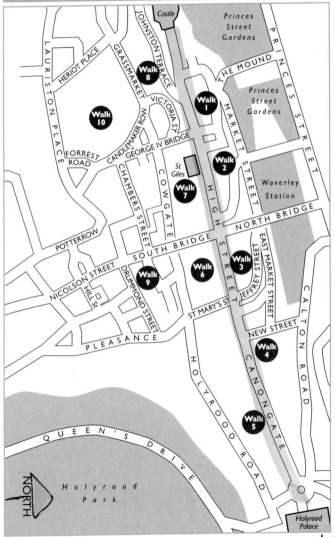

Edinburgh's Old Town

Castle

Princes Street Gardens

THE MOUND

Princes Street Gardens

JOHNSTON TERRACE

HERIOT PLACE

GRASSMARKET

Walk 8

LAURISTON PLACE

Walk 10

VICTORIA ST

CANDLEMAKER ROW

FORREST ROAD

GEORGE IV BRIDGE

Walk 1

MARKET STREET

PRINCES STREET

Waverley Station

St Giles

Walk 2

Walk 7

COWGATE

CHAMBERS STREET

POTTERROW

SOUTH BRIDGE

NORTH BRIDGE

HIGH STREET

NICOLSON STREET

DRUMMOND STREET

HILL St.

Walk 9

Walk 6

Walk 3

JEFFREY STREET

EAST MARKET STREET

PLEASANCE

ST MARY'S ST

NEW STREET

Walk 4

CANONGATE

CALTON ROAD

HOLYROOD ROAD

Walk 5

QUEEN'S DRIVE

NORTH

Holyrood Park

Holyrood Palace

East

The Development of the Old Town

To most visitors the Old Town of Edinburgh means the Royal Mile, running down from the Castle to Holyrood Palace. It is a handsome, airy street with dramatic views of the Forth estuary, Calton Hill and Arthur's Seat. It gives, however, a very misleading impression of what Edinburgh was like when the Old Town was the city and the New Town was open fields.

Gladstone's Land

Until the mid-eighteenth century, the line of the street was broken at the Netherbow Port by a fortified gate. The rest of the Royal Mile down to Holyrood formed the separate Burgh of the Canongate.

Above the Netherbow, there were further obstructions to the highway: the city guardhouse at the Tron Kirk, the Mercat Cross by St Giles, and the Weighhouse at the top of the West Bow. The Old Tolbooth and the Luckenbooths, rows of makeshift shops in the shadow of St Giles, almost closed off the street. The effect was of a series of linked piazzas rather than a through road.

How and why did the Old Town evolve into its present form?

Earliest Times

The site of Edinburgh Castle was fortified from the eleventh century and a settlement serving the king and the military garrison grew up on the ridge running down from the keep. The earliest domestic buildings that can still be seen today, however, date from the mid-sixteenth century.

Although the city had some form of defensive walls and gates throughout most of the Middle Ages, these were strengthened and extended with the Flodden Wall, completed in 1560. Designed to deter both the English and smugglers, parts of the Wall can still be seen (See Walks 5 and 10).

The Flodden Wall marked the boundary of the city, a 'herring-bone' of narrow closes enclosed by high tenements running down on either side of the ridge of the High Street. To the north, the marshes of the Nor' Loch provided a natural boundary. To the south lay the valley of the Cowgate and the less densely built slope rising to the Flodden Wall on its far side.

To the east and outside the walls lay the separate Burgh of the Canongate. The area was popular with the nobility whose larger houses, gardens and orchards stretched to the north and south Backs of the Canongate, now Calton Road and Holyrood Road respectively.

Prosperity and Enlightenment

At the start of the seventeenth century Edinburgh was the established capital of the independent kingdom of Scotland and a prosperous commercial centre. The Old Town was home to King, Court and Parliament, Church and University. New stone houses were built and older wooden structures modernised.

Following the accession of James VI to the throne of England in 1603, the Court, and with it most of the nobility, moved to London. In 1707, the Scottish Parliament voted itself out of existence by the Treaty of Union. Yet despite these apparent blows to its status Edinburgh's Old Town continued to thrive throughout the seventeenth, and even more so, during most of the eighteenth century.

This was the time of the Enlightenment, when Edinburgh, 'the Athens of the North', was one of the leading intellectual centres of Europe, if not the world. The Old Town was home to Adam Smith the economist, David Hume the philosopher and historian, the scientists Joseph Black and William Cullen and the renowned architectural family of Adam. Students from throughout the world came to train at Edinburgh's medical school.

James' Court, home to David Hume and James Boswell

The reason for this flowering of intellectual activity has been much

12

discussed. The explanation may lie partly in the close confines of the Old Town in which all classes and conditions lived literally on top of each other. Mr Amyat, the King's Chemist, claimed in about 1775 that at the Mercat Cross he could 'within a few minutes take fifty men of genius and learning by the hand'.

In the typical Old Town tenement, the ground floor might be occupied by a tradesman and his workshop. The lower floors were the prerogative of aristocrats or prosperous merchants who wished to get away from the noise and smells of the street while avoiding a steep, dark and tortuous climb. The highest floors, often seven or more storeys from the ground, were the province of servants or poorer workmen. All shared the same closes and stairs.

The result was a lively and gregarious community, but one whose living conditions were far from salubrious. Few houses had piped water, which was normally obtained from the wells which can still be seen (See Walks 3 and 7). Water was delivered to the more prosperous houses, for a fee, by cadies. They became famous as guides to the densely built and confusing closes, and the fount of all knowledge of what went on within them.

Even fewer houses had indoor sanitation and the closes doubled as sewers and cess-pits. It was forbidden to empty waste into the street till the curfew bell rang at 10pm. On that signal, many pots would be emptied with the traditional warning of 'Gardyloo!' The wise pedestrian ran for cover.

The upper classes met in the Assembly Rooms for balls

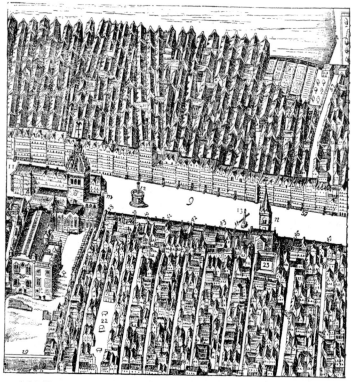

A bird's eye view of Edinburgh in 1647, with St Giles on the left

and receptions or at St Cecilia's Hall for concerts, conveyed there in sedan chairs to avoid spoiling their finery. Most social life, however, revolved around pubs or 'howffs'. There, all classes and professions could meet over a common interest in matters political, cultural or intellectual, or claret.

Emigrants and Immigrants

A shortage of building land and concerns about security combined to keep the city more or less within its traditional boundaries until after the defeat of Bonnie Prince Charlie's rebellion in 1746. Nonetheless, demand from prosperous residents for more space and privacy was gathering momentum. This could only partially be met by developments such as James' Court and Chessel's Court within the Old Town itself (see Walks 1 and 5).

In 1763, the North Bridge was built across the Nor' Loch. It breached the perimeter of the city and opened the way for the development of the spaciously planned New Town on the ridge across the valley of what is now Princes Street Gardens. With the similar and initially more successful developments to the South of the Old Town around George Square, it signalled the start of the Old Town's decline.

Slow at first, the pace of decline accelerated dramatically as the prosperous classes moved out and the poor moved in. Houses were subdivided and let to the poor who, as often as not, sublet them again to the even poorer. By the early nineteenth century the Old Town had become a dangerous and overcrowded slum. It is estimated that the population, swelled by immigrants from the Highlands and Ireland, more than quadrupled by the middle of the century. Families of seven regularly lived in one room.

Crime, prostitution and, most notoriously, drunkenness flourished. In 1829, Burke and Hare found their victims in those attracted to the 'lodging house' Burke ran in a room 16ft by 10ft in which he and his mistress also lived. They murdered the lodgers and sold their corpses to Dr Knox for dissection in his anatomy classes. As the contemporary jingle had it

> Down the close and up the stair
> But an' ben wi' Burke and Hare
> Burke's the butcher, Hare's the thief,
> Knox the man who buys the beef.

In the Canongate, where some vacant land remained, industry added its contribution of pollution and noxious odours. By 1863 there were eight breweries, three tanneries, two foundries, seven metalworks and a major gas works, not to mention 15 byres housing 135 cows in the Canongate area alone.

Most housing investment went into successive New Towns to the north of the city. Building in the Old Town, still the home of most public institutions such as the City Council and the law courts, was confined to improving access. The North Bridge was extended on the far side of the High Street with the building of South Bridge over the Cowgate in 1785. Started in 1827, George IV Bridge continued to the south the line of the Mound created from the soil dug out to lay the foundations of the New Town.

Access from the west was provided at about the same time via Johnston Terrace running up the side of the Castle Rock and Victoria Street, linking the Grassmarket with George IV Bridge. Only the need to replace the tenements between the Tron Kirk and Parliament Close, spectacularly burned down in 1824, resulted in any significant new building in the Old Town.

In 1859, Cockburn Street was driven through the closes on the North slope below the Royal Mile to provide convenient access to Waverley Station from the south. This had the added benefit of clearing some of the slums and opening up the closes to light and air.

As the century progressed, some efforts were made to draw attention to and ameliorate the condition of the poor. The Free Church of Scotland built churches and promoted paupers' missions. Dr Guthrie established Ragged Schools to give the children of the Old Town closes at least the rudiments of an education, as well as an introduction to Christianity. More advanced education was provided in the Heriot's Trust schools built about 1840 in the Cowgate and Old Assembly Close.

Pamphleteers described the horrors of life in the closes. After touring the area by night with a police escort, Dr George Bell wrote: 'In those yards and closes, whole communities are caged and generate steam, both physical and moral, that revolts both the senses and the mind.' Among his proposed solutions was a good measure of prohibition, to counter the activities of the myriad of pubs and dram sellers.

The Pioneers of Renewal

In 1861 the tenement at Paisley's Close collapsed with the loss of 35 lives. This disaster, highlighting in the most dramatic way possible the extent of overcrowding, finally spurred officialdom to action. Dr Henry Littlejohn was appointed as the city's first Medical Officer of Health.

Heave awa' lads ah'm no deid yet!

In 1865 he published his *Report on the Sanitary Condition of the City*. His painstaking statistics made stark and compelling reading. There were 646 people per acre living between North Bridge and St Mary's Street compared with 90 per acre in the New Town. The proportions of children dying before the age of five were 18% and 7% respectively. These differences were magnified during epidemics. Nearly a quarter of the population of the Grassmarket suffered in the fever epidemic of 1847-48 whereas only 0.8% of those living just across the valley in the New Town caught the disease.

Littlejohn recommended the strict enforcement of byelaws requiring the cleaning of closes and stairs, their lighting by gas, and the removal of wooden balconies and other structures from buildings. Many of these must already have collapsed. He suggested paving the closes so that they could be effectively drained and washed. There should be more public toilets, although perhaps surprisingly Littlejohn was against the installation of WCs in the tenements, believing that the tenants would not keep them clean.

The next major phase of rebuilding was promoted by Patrick Geddes in the Lawnmarket. While lecturing in zoology at Edinburgh University, Geddes pioneered the scientific approach to the relationship between individuals and their urban environment. His work has earned him the title of 'Father of Town Planning'. He was also a romantic and enthusiast, who believed that the eighteenth-century Old Town, where all classes lived together in one community, was a desirable and regainable ideal.

In 1887, with his new wife, he moved to James' Court, then a slum, and proceeded to inspire the repair and redevelopment of the area. He bought Short's Observatory, now the Outlook Tower, converting it into a museum and 'sociological laboratory' to promote his ideas. He persuaded the University to renovate some of the properties to provide residences for 120 students. He built Ramsay Garden as flats for professors and lecturers in a style that reflected his romantic image of how the Old Town should look.

Geddes' vision of a true community of scholars in the Old Town was not followed through after his departure from Edinburgh. He did, however, sow the seeds of the idea that the Old Town is a good place to live and work, an idea that has taken nearly a century to come to fruition.

Revival Gathers Pace

At the start of the twentieth century, the City Council began to clear the slums and provide decent housing. Tron Square and Portsburgh Square, solid blocks of flats with balconies and open space for drying greens and playgrounds, replaced some of the worst slums. This programme continued after the First World War when E J Macrae, the City Architect, built a number of tenements in a characteristic, rather grim, Scots baronial style. The Greyfriars Hotel in Cowgatehead is a surviving example.

Inevitably, clearing the slums led to a drop in population, a trend that accelerated after 1945. With its emphasis on functional zones, post-War planning was totally at variance with the spirit of the Old Town, where all kinds of activities took place in the same area or even in the same building. The planners zoned most of the Old Town for 'cultural and recreational' activities, although the Canongate was to remain residential

Roads formed another threat. A 'Bridges Relief Road' of six lanes was planned on the line of St Mary's Street. It would have meant a final and fatal breach in the enclosure of the Royal Mile, as well as the demolition of some of the better housing. Fortunately, it was never built.

More sympathetically, the drive for housing improvement intensified. In many Old Town tenements, people still lived in one room and shared a WC with several other families. For a bath or clothes washing, they had to head for Infirmary Street baths or one of the local 'steamies'.

It is more questionable whether the City Council's solution of moving large numbers of people out to high-rise flats on the edge of the city with few amenities, was the right one. Although the prospect of better housing was initially tempting, many of the Old Town residents who moved very soon wished to return. At the same time, depopulation in the Old Town was severe. In 1971, for example, the population of the Grassmarket area was only a third of what it had been in 1951. Inevitably, lack of people also meant the loss of amenities such as food shops and public transport.

Given the circumstances it is perhaps surprising that more damage was not done. In the Canongate some houses were rebuilt sympathetically, improving the housing but retaining the scale and feel of the street. Some seriously intrusive large scale developments did occur in the 1960s and 1970s, including the local government offices on the corner of the Lawnmarket and George IV Bridge, the government offices in Jeffrey Street and the Heriot-Watt University building in the Grassmarket, the last two now converted into hotels. Already, most of these buildings have outlived their original purpose.

At the end of the sixties, reaction set in with a renewed appreciation of the value of city-centre living. Fortunately, enough of the local community remained to take action. Housing associations were set up using government finance to rehabilitate the tenements. The people who had been moved out to the new estates started to come back.

Private developers followed the lead of the housing associations. Initially, they built tiny 'studio flats', derided by locals as 'single ends', the traditional term for one-room living. Gradually, they discovered that there was also a market for higher quality accommodation. Between 1981 and 1991, the population of the Old Town virtually doubled and has continued to rise.

The Old Town Today

The Old Town is once more a varied and vigorous community. Families who have lived here for generations have been joined by students and young professionals who enjoy city-centre living. Large-scale industry, most notably the gas works and the giant Holyrood Brewery, has moved out, leaving major sites for redevelopment, culminating in the the new Scottish Parliament building, now under construction.

While the Courts, local government and the University remain large employers and some small professional offices have set up business here, the main economic activity is now tourism. The integration of visitors' needs with the desires of local residents is not without its problems. Tour buses and late-night drinking cause disturbance, and woollen mills may be able to afford higher rents than local shops, but on the whole the balance works.

In order to promote this diversity and maintain the balance between the interests of resident and tourist, business and developer, a partnership of public bodies including Lothian and Edinburgh Enterprise Ltd backed the work of the Edinburgh Old Town Renewal Trust. Under its guidance, the Old Town of Edinburgh continued to develop, but its development was sympathetically managed.

Developments ranged from replacing the paving in some of the closes to making the Royal Mile a more pleasant place in which to stroll or watch the world go by. In 1997, the Old and New Towns of Edinburgh were added to the list of UNESCO World Heritage Sites, in recognition of their unique quality and interest as models of urban development. The Old Town Renewal Trust merged with its New Town equivalent to form the Edinburgh World Heritage Trust.

Paradoxically, most of the fabric of the Old Town is actually newer than the New Town. Yet the constraints of its geography and the intricate land ownership mean that the Old Town has retained its traditional character of diversity, contrasting strikingly with the elegant uniformity of the New Town.

The following walks through the network of closes, entries, wynds and courts will give you a feel for what the Old Town must have been like during its various stages of development. Fortunately, most of the authentic smells have gone, but the ghosts of the past still linger. Listen carefully and you may still hear the carousers in the howffs or the cries of the cadies.

Walk 1

SOLDIERS, MINISTERS AND PRIME MINISTERS

The Castle Esplanade to Bank Street

Starting from the Castle Esplanade, the walk takes you down Ramsay Lane, with fine views over the city, to the Assembly Halls, the temporary home of the Scottish Parliament, and then through some of the Old Town's most attractive closes. These owe much to Patrick Geddes, who pioneered the revival of the Old Town in the late nineteenth century. His 'restoration' added a greater degree of picturesqueness than the Old Town ever had.

There are plenty of distractions on this fairly level route. You can choose to climb the Outlook Tower with its Camera Obscura, experience the lifestyle of a seventeenth-century merchant in Gladstone's Land, listen to a parliamentary debate or visit the Writers' Museum with its memorabilia of Robert Burns, Sir Walter Scott and Robert Louis Stevenson. You can even buy a tartan rug or a Shetland shawl, as this area round the castle is a Mecca for tourist shoppers.

Route

Start at the entry to the Esplanade, with your back to the

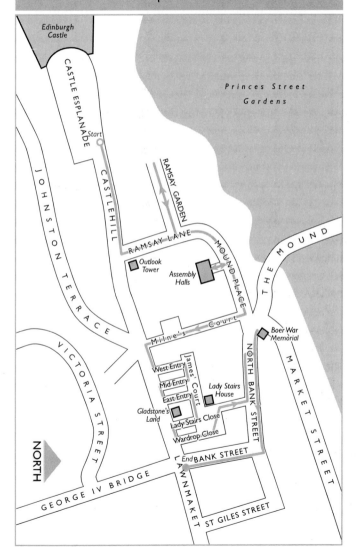

Walk 1 The Castle Esplanade to Bank Street

Edinburgh Castle

CASTLE ESPLANADE

CASTLEHILL

JOHNSTON TERRACE

Start

RAMSAY GARDEN

RAMSAY LANE

Princes Street Gardens

Outlook Tower

Assembly Halls

MOUND PLACE

THE MOUND

Milne's Court

Boer War Memorial

VICTORIA STREET

NORTH

West Entry

Mid Entry

East Entry

James' Court

Lady Stairs House

Gladstone's Land

Lady Stairs Close

Wardrop Close

NORTH BANK STREET

MARKET STREET

End BANK STREET

LAWNMARKET

GEORGE IV BRIDGE

ST GILES STREET

Castle. Ahead is the gentle slope of Castlehill, the first of the four streets that together make up the length of the Royal Mile. On your left, overlooking the Esplanade, is Patrick Geddes's masterpiece, Ramsay Garden, a nineteenth-century romantic vision of medieval Edinburgh. With spacious rooms and superb views, secluded yet very central, these flats are still the most desirable properties in the Old Town.

Against the wall ahead of you is a curious Art Nouveau fountain, commemorating the witches burnt at the stake on the Esplanade. The witches in Shakespeare's *Macbeth* reflect a periodic Scottish obsession, with serious consequences for some old women who had upset their neighbours.

Witches Well

Patrick Geddes, 'the father of Town Planning' was the driving force behind the late nineteenth-century revival of the top of the Old Town. Here, he sought to recreate the spirit of intellectual creativity that prevailed in the Old Town during the eighteenth-century Enlighten-ment. He partially realised his vision of a close-knit academic community with Ramsay Garden housing the professors and the surrounding tenements being restored for students.

Head down Castlehill. On your left is not a fortification but the water tank built in 1850 to store the water supply for the city, now converted into a weaving workshop where visitors can watch tartan being made.

Turn left into Ramsay Lane. Opposite is the Outlook Tower, which still houses the Camera Obscura of 1853, a system of mirrors and lenses that projects images of the surrounding scene onto a viewing table. You can have great fun watching people picnicking in Princes Street Gardens or running for a bus, as well as the chance to view Edinburgh's buildings from unusual angles. At the top of the tower there is a viewing gallery with panoramic views over Edinburgh. The Outlook Tower also houses an exhibition of holograms and other optical illusions.

Near the foot of Ramsay Lane turn left to reach the courtyard of Geddes' Ramsay Garden, past a row of eighteenth-century houses whose steps and balconies are a riot of colour in summer. On the right as you stand in the courtyard are the remaining pilasters of the distinctive octagonal house built by Allan Ramsay, the poet, around 1740. Its unusual shape gave it the nickname, Goose Pie House. Look on the building ahead for the cherubs masquerading as farmer, mason and blacksmith, and the dragon.

Leaving Ramsay Garden, turn left and follow the lane round to the right. There is a fine view over Princes Street Gardens to the New Town with the Firth of Forth and the coastline of Fife in the distance.

Ramsay Lane changes into Mound Place, the centre of much of Scotland's religious life. On the right are New College, the Theology Faculty of Edinburgh University, and the Assembly Halls, the annual meeting place of the General Assembly of the Church of Scotland and now the temporary home of the Scottish Parliament.

The **Assembly Halls** were built by the Free Church of Scotland, established after 487 ministers walked out of the General Assembly of 1843. They were protesting at the right of the lay proprietor of the parish, usually the local landowner, to appoint the minister rather than the church congregation.

The Assembly Halls were erected by the new Church leaders on as prominent a site as could be imagined, obscuring the meeting place of the established Church. This was in the Highland Tolbooth Church, now converted into the headquarters of the Edinburgh International Festival, whose spire dominates the top of the Royal Mile. Indeed, the Halls were said to add insult to injury by 'stealing' the church's spire. From Princes Street, the spire of the Highland Tolbooth looks as if it belongs to the Assembly Halls.

Most of the Free Church reunited with the Church of Scotland in 1928 after lay patronage was abandoned, and this explains why it is now the Church of Scotland that holds its annual Assembly in the Halls. In 1999, the halls became the temporary home of the Scottish Parliament while its permanent premises are built at Holyrood.

On the left side of the courtyard of the Assembly Halls you can see a statue of John Knox, leader of the Scottish Reformation. This compensates somewhat for the neglect of his grave, which now lies under a parking space on the south side of St Giles (*See Walk 7*).

Just past the Assembly Halls, turn up the flight of steps leading through an arch into **Milne's Court**. This is the first real close of the walk. An atmospheric example it is too, with three underpasses, steps and high tenements closing it in. The tenements, originally built by Robert Mylne (or

Milne) in 1690, were restored in 1969 as student residences. The public entrance to the Scottish Parliament opens off Milne's Court.

Note the turret staircases, crow-step gables and windows with wooden shutters on their lower half, traditionally a cheaper way of keeping out the fierce east winds than glass. These features are all characteristic of older Scottish domestic architecture. You will see many examples as you explore the closes of the Old Town.

Go through the arch or pend at the top of Milne's Court to rejoin the Royal Mile, at this point called the Lawnmarket, and turn left past a Victorian pillar box and one of the city's kiltmakers. Take the unimaginatively named **West Entry** left into **James' Court**.

The walk now snakes in and out of the closes into James' Court. The tenement facing you was built by James Brownhill in the 1720s to meet demand from the professional classes for more spacious accommodation. In the short time that it served this purpose before losing its clientele to the New Town, it was home to David Hume, the historian and philosopher, and to James Boswell, who entertained Dr Johnson in his flat here. Now the Court is once more a desirable place to live.

Return to the Lawnmarket by **Mid Entry** and turn left. Just past the next close is Gladstone's Land, with a golden bird on its sign. At one time, most tradesmen in the Old Town would advertise their premises with an illustrated sign, to reflect their particular trade and to guide those who could not read.

At one time, **Gladstone's Land** belonged to the ancestors of W E Gladstone, the nineteenth-century Liberal Prime Minister. He was MP for Midlothian, the constituency that included Edinburgh, in the latter part of his career. Gladstone's Land has been restored by the National Trust for Scotland as a typical seventeenth-century merchant's house with a street-level arcade, preserved ceiling paintings, and, perhaps more conjecturally, a model pig lying in front of the shop door. This recalls the time when pigs regularly foraged in the closes, despite repeated attempts by the Town Council to fine their owners.

Go down **East Entry**. On your left is the Jolly Judge pub, with reconstructed painted ceilings and a welcoming fire in winter. Turn sharp right round the back of Gladstone's Land where there are old door lintels and a fine wooden staircase.

Return to the Lawnmarket by **Lady Stair's Close**. Above the close mouth on the Lawnmarket side, you will find a plaque commemorating the poet Robert Burns's first visit to Edinburgh in 1786. At your feet, yet another plaque! This one, simply marking a good spot to take a photo, can be found in several places around the Old Town.

*Dragon at
Wardrop's Close*

Turn left down the Lawnmarket and left again through **Wardrop's Close**. The tenement above the close mouth is another example of Patrick Geddes at work. Look for the heads representing the arts, sciences and crafts under the oriel windows that face the Lawnmarket. His green and blue dragons at the close mouth are a nice touch, though the appearance of the close is not helped by its yellow tiles.

This close recalls another Geddes. On the left of the close mouth, you can still make out the words, 'Geddes ... binders', a reminder of Edinburgh's position in the nineteenth century as a major publishing centre.

Lady Stair's House

On your left across the court is Lady Stair's House, now the Writers' Museum, celebrating the lives of three of Scotland's greatest authors, Robert Burns, Sir Walter Scott, and Robert Louis Stevenson. Originally built in 1622, the house was restored and presented to the city by Lord Rosebery, another nineteenth-century Liberal Prime Minister with local connections. The plaque on the wall records his generosity. Facing you is Blackie House, a particularly fine example of seventeenth-century Scots domestic architecture.

Cross the court diagonally and go down the steps at the side of Lady Stair's House to reach Bank Street. Poetic

31

quotations carved into the paving stones and the distinctive emblem on the modern gates of Makars' Court continue the theme of the Writers' Museum.

Turn left and cross Bank Street at the pedestrian crossing a few yards down. The large statue to your left commemorates the soldiers of the Black Watch Regiment who died in the Boer War. From here you have a good view of the Old Town skyline and the eight- or nine-storey tenements, whose height was dictated by its confined space.

Return up Bank Street past the front of the headquarters of the Bank of Scotland, a boldly conceived and opulent palace to money. As an institution, the Bank is only three years younger than the Bank of England. Ironically, although the Bank of England was founded by a Scot, the driving force behind the Bank of Scotland was an Englishman.

Cross St Giles Street and make your way up Bank Street past the new extension to the High Court. Look out for a blue plaque on the tenement across the street. It marks the original TB clinic of Sir Robert Philip. He established the means of managing the transmission of the disease, a method that has saved countless lives throughout the world.

The walk ends at the traffic lights on the intersection of the Lawnmarket with Bank Street and George IV Bridge. Turn round for a splendid view of the Bank building topped by the gilded statue of the Golden Boy, symbolising Fame.

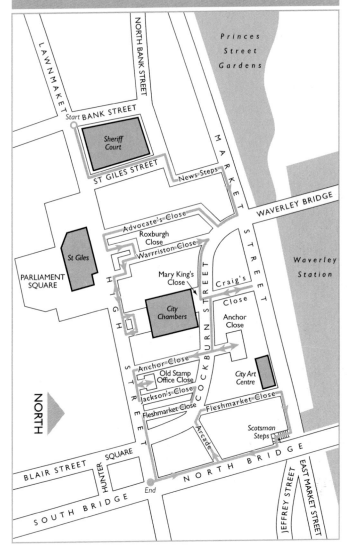

Walk 2 Bank Street to North Bridge

LAWNMARKET

NORTH BANK STREET

Princes Street Gardens

Start BANK STREET

Sheriff Court

ST GILES STREET

News Steps

MARKET STREET

WAVERLEY BRIDGE

Advocate's Close

Roxburgh Close

Warrriston Close

St Giles

HIGH

PARLIAMENT SQUARE

Mary King's Close

City Chambers

Craig's Close

Anchor Close

COCKBURN STREET

Waverley Station

STREET

Anchor Close

Old Stamp Office Close

City Art Centre

STREET

Jackson's Close

Fleshmarket Close

Fleshmarket Close

NORTH

Arcade

Scotsman Steps

BLAIR STREET

HUNTER SQUARE

End

NORTH BRIDGE

JEFFREY STREET

EAST MARKET STREET

SOUTH BRIDGE

Walk 2

ADVOCATES, COUNCILLORS AND JOURNALISTS

Bank Street to North Bridge

This walk is one of the most energetic, descending and ascending the slope three times by some of the longest and most dramatic closes.

Starting from the top of the Mound on the Royal Mile, it takes you down the News Steps and up Advocate's Close, one of the most picturesque in the Old Town. After visiting the City Chambers you descend by Warriston Close to Cockburn Street, a Victorian development designed to give access to the Old Town from the railway station.

After visiting two closes below Cockburn Street you ascend by the narrow Anchor Close to visit three more and an arcade off the High Street. The final descent via the busy Fleshmarket Close is followed by a stiff climb up the Scotsman Steps to look out over North Bridge before returning to the High Street.

Route

Start at the corner of Bank Street and the Royal Mile, outside the former Sheriff Court, now remodelled as an extension to the High Court. A recent statue celebrates the philosopher, David Hume. Look across and down the street for a fine view of Parliament Square, St Giles and the Tron Kirk with the hills of Fife visible in the distance on a clear day.

Walk down the High Street and turn first left into St Giles Street. Note the street names which indicate that this street, not the broader George IV Bridge, marks the change from the Lawnmarket to the High Street.

Proceed to the corner where the street bends to the left. There is a fine view over Princes Street to the gothic Scott Monument and Calton Hill crowned by an unfinished replica of the Parthenon.

Go through the gate facing you and down the steep News Steps, a reminder that the printing works of the *Evening News* used to be nearby. At the bottom turn right. On the next corner is the Traveline Office, open from 8.30 am to 4.30 pm on weekdays, which provides information on Edinburgh's bus services.

Turn right into Cockburn Street and then right again up the steps into **Advocate's Close**. After the first flight you pass on your left the blocked-off entrance to **Roxburgh Close**.

Pass under a building, turn to the left and ascend the close. Although advocates, the Scots equivalent of barristers, use it in going from the station to the Courts, Advocate's Close is actually called after a former Lord Advocate, Sir James Stewart, who lived here at the end of the seventeenth century.

After passing some unremarkable buildings, note the inscription over the ornate Victorian doorway on the left. Under the initials CW and the date 1882, there is the inscription 'He that tholes overcomes', the motto of the brothers William and Robert Chambers, whose publishing works occupied the area between here and Warriston Close in the nineteenth century.

To thole is a Scots word meaning to endure suffering and recalls the hard times the **Chambers** brothers endured when their father lost his job, forcing them to make their own way in the world in their early teens. After serving an apprenticeship, William started in business as a printer and publisher. Robert joined him, writing many of the works that they published, including in 1825 *Traditions of Old Edinburgh*, a fascinating collection of history and anecdote much admired by Sir Walter Scott.

They went on to publish *Chambers Edinburgh Journal* and in 1856 *Chambers Encyclopedia*. Robert also has a place in the history of science as the author of the anonymously published *Vestiges of Creation*, a best-seller which in 1844 advocated the theory of evolution. Though of little scientific merit, Darwin welcomed it as paving the way for his more serious exposition which was eventually published in 1859. The firm continues to publish dictionaries and reference works to this day.

The buildings on the right side of the close were demolished in 1883. There are now open views down to the Scott Monument, and up to the backs of the six-storey-high houses with traditional stair towers on the High Street.

Beyond the cleared site in the now inaccessible **Byres Close** can be seen a wing of a house with semicircular pediments above the top-floor windows. This house is traditionally associated with Adam Bothwell, the Bishop of Orkney, who married Mary Queen of Scots to Bothwell. It was, however, built about 1630, well after his death!

On the left near the top of the close you can see some old lintels inscribed with dates, initials and mottoes reset in the wall.

On reaching the High Street turn left. Turn left again into the recently reopened upper part of **Roxburgh Close** to reach a paved square set with birch trees surrounded by metal grilles with astronomical designs in relief and some welcome seats. Go across the square and turn right

The Royal Exchange, now the City Chambers

up Warriston Close to return to the High Street, turning left to reach the City Chambers. Built in the 1750s as a merchants' exchange, to a design by John Adam, it never really worked. The merchants preferred to continue to meet in the High Street and Parliament Close. In the nineteenth century the building was taken over and expanded by the City Council as its headquarters.

Note the plaque on the wall on the left as you enter the quadrangle in front of the City Chambers, commemorating Mary Queen of Scots' last night in Edinburgh. Under the arcade lies the City War Memorial, a simple stone designed by Sir Edwin Lutyens and unveiled in 1928 by Prince Henry, later Duke of Gloucester.

In the middle of the courtyard there is a statue of Alexander and his horse Bucephalus by John Steell who was also responsible for the statue of the Duke of Wellington outside Register House. Though modelled in 1832 it was not actually cast till 1883.

Turn and retrace your steps down **Warriston Close**, continuing to its foot. This is a distinctly dull close; wide, bordered by Council offices and crossed by an ugly overpass. The top part of the close before the bend to the left is **Writers' Court**, where the library of the Writers to the Signet, or solicitors, now in Parliament Close, used to be.

At the bottom of the close cross Cockburn Street and turn right. Cockburn Street was cut through the closes in 1859 not only to provide access from the High Street to the station, but also as a conscious slum-clearance measure. The Scots baronial buildings were designed to retain the romantic character of the Old Town while improving standards. The street is named after Lord Cockburn.

Lord Cockburn was a leading lawyer and conservationist in the early nineteenth century. His *Memorials* give a vivid and amusing picture of the life and characters in Edinburgh during the eighteenth century Enlightenment. He led the campaign to maintain Princes Street Gardens as an open space, and gave his name to the Cockburn Association, Edinburgh's main conservation body.

Go past the Stills Gallery, which holds regular photography exhibitions, and look across the street. The high rear wall of the City Chambers rises in a steep cliff to an elaborate top storey. **Mary King's Close**, which had been walled up after the inhabitants died of plague, was 'buried' in the foundations of the Chambers. It still exists as it was in the sixteenth century, complete with ghost. It can be visited on guided walks: look out for information boards in the High Street.

Turn left down **Craig's Close**, steep and narrow particularly at the bottom end. After descending as far as you wish, return to Cockburn Street.

Continue up Cockburn Street and take the next left into **Anchor Close**. This ends in a platform and a seat overlooking Market Street and Waverley Station with a view across to Princes Street and the five-star Balmoral Hotel. You may even hear a train announced. The site below is scheduled for re-development, and is to include a hands-on science centre.

Return to Cockburn Street, cross and continue up Anchor Close, named after the Anchor tavern, the pub or howff frequented by the Crochallan Fencibles. This was perhaps the most famous of the eighteenth-century dining clubs because Burns was a member. Steep and enclosed but with not much to see, the close was home to Walter Scott's parents before they moved to the New Town and the site of the first publication of the *Encyclopaedia Britannica* in 1771.

At the top turn left down the High Street, passing the gated closes, **Geddes Entry** and **North Foulis Close**. Note the plaque to James Gillespie, snuffmaker and founder of a school that still exists.

Go into **Old Stamp Office Close**, where a low-level barrier closes off a pleasant courtyard which serves as a play area for the Royal Mile Nursery. Only the steel chimney ducts of the adjoining restaurants detract from the scene.

Old Stamp Office Close

Return to and continue down the High Street. Note the plaque above Costa Coffee to Elsie Inglis, a pioneer of women's medicine.

Pass, or for completeness, explore the dead-end **Lyons Close** and turn left into **Jackson's Close** where a board on the side of a pub tells the story of Jenny Geddes, who threw her stool at the preacher in protest at Charles I's attempt to introduce the Prayer Book. Go down as far as Cockburn Street, turn right and return to the High Street by **Fleshmarket Close**. With their narrow passages lined with houses and pubs, these closes, though now cut short by Cockburn Street, retain their Old Town atmosphere.

At the top of Fleshmarket Close turn left, cross Cockburn Street and after a few yards turn left into North Bridge. Walk down to reach the entrance of the **Arcade**, an example of a Victorian shopping mall. With most of the shop fronts modernised, it retains little of its Victorian character.

Follow the Arcade through to Cockburn Street, turn right, and then right again down the lower section of Fleshmarket Close. A convenient short cut to the station, this close is quite lively, with shops and two pubs on the left and the former *Scotsman* newspaper offices, now a luxury hotel, on the right. It led originally down to the Fleshmarket, which was situated on the side of the Nor' Loch to facilitate waste disposal.

At the foot of the close the City Art Centre and the Fruitmarket Gallery, which each house frequent exhibitions and a cafe, lie to the left.

Turn right for a few yards and enter the foot of the **Scots-man Steps**, a semi-enclosed spiral of stairs leading back up to North Bridge. Somehow the enclosed stairs with limited views make it seem a much harder climb than an ordinary close!

On reaching North Bridge, turn left and walk a few paces onto the bridge. North Bridge was the first breach in the integrity of the Old Town through which, at the end of the eighteenth century, its wealth and quality leaked away to the open spaces of the New Town.

There is a fine view over and across the valley in both directions. Note the classical Register House, by Robert Adam, at the head of the bridge. On the slopes of Calton Hill to the right, the monumental 1930s building is St Andrew's House, headquarters of the Scottish Executive, the seat of the Government in Scotland. An appropriate use is now awaited for the classical former High School just above it, once tipped as the seat of the Scottish Parliament. Below lie the roofs of Waverley station.

Return up North Bridge to reach the High Street again and the end of the walk.

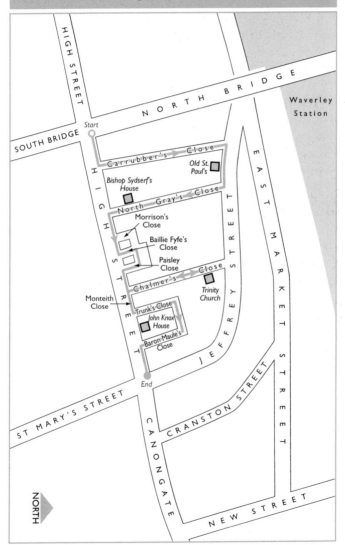

Walk 3
BISHOPS, REFORMERS AND SURVIVORS

North Bridge to Jeffrey Street

This walk has a religious theme. It takes you down past the site of an Archbishop's house to Old St Paul's Church. The ascent of North Gray's Close past a Bishop's house is followed by Baillie Fyfe's Close with a view of a veritable urban jungle! Paisley Close was the scene of a miraculous escape. Down Chalmers Close you pass Carrubber's Mission to reach Trinity Apse, returning to John Knox's house.

Trunk's Close leads to a charming hidden garden. Finally you come to the site of the Netherbow Port, the old gate that marked the end of the city of Edinburgh—or, in the view of the citizens, the World's End.

Route

From the corner of North Bridge and the High Street, turn down the High Street, and left into **Carrubber's Close**, a wide, well-paved close with bollards down the middle. This leads past the back of the Carlton Highland Hotel. A plaque on the right marks the site of the house

44

of Archbishop Spottiswood, Archbishop of St Andrews, who crowned Charles I at Holyrood in 1633.

Further down on the right is the late nineteenth-century Old St Paul's Episcopal Church, its bell silhouetted against the sky. The church is the home of the oldest Episcopal congregation in Scotland. It first met in a wool store on this site after being expelled from St Giles in 1689.

At the bottom of the close, with its archway dated 1899, turn right past the church door. The front is graced by an enormous crucifix. The remarkable large and attractive interior dating from 1890-1905 is worth a visit. Outside, a bench provides a fine view over to Calton Hill.

Continue past the church and turn right up **North Gray's Close**. This close is narrow, unevenly paved and rather rural with ivy cascading over the wall on the left. On the right, near the top, after passing a modern bay window look out for the ruins of Bishop Sydserf's House dating from 1581. If you step through the door you can see the base of a spiral stair to the left.

Continue through the narrow entry at the top of the close. Looking back up the High Street you will see that the tenements have been cut down to two storeys, leaving an ugly gap in the frontage which may one day be restored to its original height.

Turn left down the High Street passing the gated **Morrison's Close**, and turn left again into **Baillie Fyfe's Close**. The pend leads into a small courtyard. Go up the steps facing you. Over the wall you will see a large expanse of jungle concealing the site of a former tannery. In season it is a mass of flowering buddleia much loved by butterflies. Returning, note the almost indecipherable carved stone over the door under the steps.

Turn to the right across the court and return to the High Street by the pend at the other end, **Paisley Close**. Over the entrance to the close there is the carved head of a boy with the inscription 'Heave awa' chaps, I'm no dead yet.'

Paisley Close inscription

This commemorates the lad's escape from the collapse of a tenement in 1861 in which 35 people were killed. He is reported to have called out these words to the rescuers searching the ruins, although it does seem unlikely that an Edinburgh tenement-dweller would use the word 'chaps'.

The accident drew attention to the appalling overcrowding in the Old Town tenements. It led to the appointment of the city's first Medical Officer of Health and the institution of a programme of improvements.

Turn left down the High Street and then left into **Chalmers Close**. This close is not particularly attractive, leading into the carpark of a 1960s government office block, recently re-fronted as a hotel. It is worth going down, however, to see on the right near the bottom the reconstructed Trinity College Church, now a brass rubbing centre.

Trinity College Church and Hospital was founded in 1460 by Queen Mary of Gueldres in memory of her husband, James II of Scotland, who was killed at the siege of Roxburgh when one of his own cannon exploded. It included a handsome church in Gothic style. The altar-piece from this church is one of the treasures of the National Gallery of Scotland on the Mound.

At the Reformation the College was taken over by the City Council and used as a parish church until 1848 when it was demolished to make way for Waverley Station. As a condition of the sale the railway company paid for the church to be taken apart and all the stones numbered, so that it could be re-erected on another site. Before a site was agreed in 1872, however, many stones had been pilfered, permitting only a choir to be re-erected, as part of a modern Gothic church.

That church was in turn demolished in 1959 to make way for the government offices, leaving only the apse. Despite its strange history, it is a noble and richly decorated Gothic interior. It can be visited free during the opening hours of the Brass Rubbing Centre.

Returning to the High Street, turn left past Carrubbers Close Mission. Confusingly, this handsome pillared building is not in Carrubbers Close.

Continue past gated **Monteith Close**. One of the characteristic Old Town wells stands on the pavement opposite the entrance. These wells provided the only water supply to the city. The dent in the stonework under the tap, hammered out by thousands of buckets, can still be seen. The wells have recently been restored, including plumbing to allow them to produce water again!

Ahead you will see Moubray House and John Knox's House, the latter open to the public. Dating from the sixteenth century, these are among the oldest, and certainly the most picturesque, houses in the Old Town. Note the inscriptions and carvings on the overhanging upper storeys. The connection with John Knox, the leader of the Scottish Reformation, is somewhat uncertain!

Just before reaching Moubray House turn left into **Trunk's Close** with its contemporary metalwork gate which is unfortunately locked

John Knox House carving of Moses

outside working hours. This close is a pleasant, rather rustic passage, down the side of Moubray House. At the bottom on the right are the offices of the Cockburn Association.

The **Cockburn Association** takes its name from Lord Cockburn (see Walk 2), who led the protest against proposals to build on Princes Street Gardens. Founded in 1875 the Cockburn is Edinburgh's most influential conservation society. It comments on all proposed developments in the city, campaigning against the demolition of historic buildings and promoting their restoration and re-use. Depending on one's point of view, its vigorous campaigning is sometimes credited with, or blamed for, the absence in Edinburgh of any large-scale road building.

At the foot of Trunk's Close lies a surprise—a well cared for garden, with a bold metal sculpture of a cock. The building ahead is the office of an architectural practice.

Follow the path to the right through the garden, round the back of the houses to **Baron Maule's Close** and return to the High Street. Unfortunately the gate here is sometimes locked. If it is, you have no option but to return the way you came, turning left at the top of Trunk's Close to reach Baron Maule's Close by the High Street.

Carving of Netherbow Port

At the top of Baron Maule's Close look to the right to see the Netherbow Theatre, a centre run by the Church of Scotland. Its hanging sign shows a stylised representation of the Netherbow Port. As well as the theatre, the centre shows occasional exhibitions and houses a friendly cafe with outside seating in summer.

Continue down the High Street to the crossroads. In the roadway you will notice brass studs marking the site of the Netherbow, the original main gate of the city. It was a handsome edifice with two round towers and a square clock tower above the gate. There is a carving showing what it looked like high on the wall on your left.

The Netherbow Port was demolished in 1764 because it obstructed the road and slowed the traffic. It is ironic that the recent alterations to the High Street include the introduction of 'traffic calming' measures—restrictions and narrowing of the roadway—to slow the traffic.

You have now reached the end of the old City of Edinburgh, popularly known, with metropolitan arrogance, as the 'World's End'. The name is commemorated in the pub opposite. Beyond lies the once separate burgh of Canongate, which you can explore in Walks 4 and 5.

Walk 4 Jeffrey Street to Holyrood

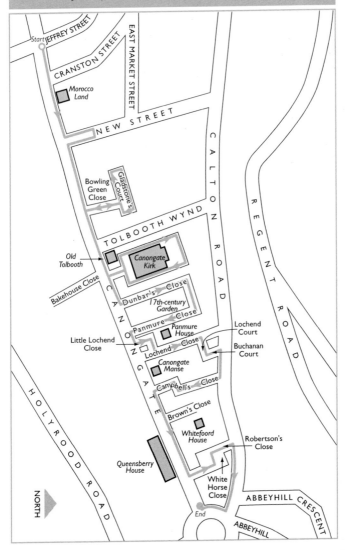

Start JEFFREY STREET

CRANSTON STREET

EAST MARKET STREET

Morocco Land

NEW STREET

CALTON ROAD

REGENT ROAD

Bowling Green Close

Gladstone's Court

TOLBOOTH WYND

Old Tolbooth

Canongate Kirk

Bakehouse Close

C A N O N G A T E

Dunbar's Close

17th-century Garden

Panmure Close

Panmure House

Lochend Court

Little Lochend Close

Lochend Close

Buchanan Court

Canongate Manse

Campbell's Close

Brown's Close

Whitefoord House

Robertson's Close

Queensberry House

White Horse Close

HOLYROOD ROAD

NORTH

ABBEYHILL CRESCENT

ABBEYHILL

End

Walk 4
MOORS, POETS AND PALFREYS

Jeffrey Street to Holyrood

This walk is relatively easy, mainly downhill with no serious climbs and several opportunities for a seat. There are fewer closes but it is none the less a pleasant route.

After strolling down the Canongate to the Tolbooth, you visit the Canongate Kirkyard and a delightful reconstructed seventeenth-century garden. A close under a modern tenement leads to an old brewery on Calton Road. You return to the Canongate to visit the very picturesque, if hardly authentic, White Horse Close.

Route

Starting at the corner of Jeffrey Street and the Royal Mile, head down the Royal Mile. From here Leith Wynd ran along the east wall of the city connecting Edinburgh to its port in Leith. You have now left the historic city of Edinburgh and are entering the former separate burgh of Canongate.

Beyond the Netherbow Port lay the burgh of **Canongate** under the jurisdiction of the Abbot and Canons of Holyrood

Abbey. At the Reformation in 1561, it was acquired by the Earl of Roxburgh from whom the Edinburgh Council purchased it in 1636.

Developed later and less densely than the area within the walls, the Canongate was a place where the court nobility built large houses up to the Union of the Crowns. It remained a fashionable area until the development of the New Town. Industry then moved in, including a gas works, breweries and eventually a bus garage.

Most of its housing was restored or rebuilt from the 1950s on, in more or less traditional style. More recently, the industrial sites have been abandoned and some brewery buildings have been converted to housing. New Street Bus Station is planned to become housing, with a hotel and arts centre.

Look down Cranston Street for a view across the valley to the Governor's House of the former Calton Prison, a picturesquely castellated building. On the right down Cranston Street is the hall where the likes of Dudley Moore and Alan Bennett first made their name in the Festival Fringe.

Pass a characteristic blue former police box and the Edinburgh School of English in a converted church with its modern unicorn sign. At the gated **Midcommon Close**, look up to see on the right a small statue of a moor on the facade of Morocco Land.

Moor statue on Morocco Land

The statue and the name **Morocco Land** commemorate a merchant who made his fortune in that country.

According to legend Andrew Grey, the son of the Master of Grey, broke out of jail on the eve of his execution for rioting. Having made his fortune in Morocco, he returned as a pirate to hold Edinburgh to ransom during the last outbreak of the plague in 1645.

He took the Provost's daughter as hostage, and then having cured her of the plague, married her. He settled in the Canongate because he had sworn in exile never to return to Edinburgh. In writing *Old and New Edinburgh* James Grant confirmed the story—to the extent that the first recorded owner of the Land was called Grey!

Continue down the Canongate, past a restored arcade of shops, to New Street. At the end of New Street, through a doorway under the railway bridge, there is a flight of steps up Calton Hill.

This walk, however, continues down the Canongate. Most of the tenements along this stretch were restored or rebuilt in the 1950s and 1960s, many by Robert Hurd and Partners. In many cases the facades have been retained. They represent an early and generally successful attempt at modernisation of substandard property while retaining the essential character of the area.

As you pass, look out for interesting armorial and inscribed stones on Cordiner's Land, formerly belonging to the shoemakers', or cordiners', guild and on Bible Land carved with biblical texts. The texts are more easily seen from the other side of the street.

Turn left into **Gladstone's Court**. The backs of the

tenements, with their traditional turnpike stairs and washing poles, can be seen. The inner court houses the offices of a design company.

Return to the Canongate and turn left to reach **Tolbooth Wynd**. A little way down the Wynd on the right you can see a former well with a modern metalwork door. Across and above Tolbooth Wynd stands the Canongate Tolbooth. It now houses The People's Story, a museum of the social history of Edinburgh and well worth a visit.

Tollbooth clock

The Tolbooth, the 'town hall' of the Canongate, was built in 1591, the large clock being installed in 1884. On the front of the Tolbooth with the arms of the Burgh and its motto are carved the names of the men of the Canongate who died in the First World War: three closely packed columns. This gives some idea of the number of people who lived here in the early twentieth century.

Continue a few yards down the Canongate to the Canongate Kirk.

Canongate Kirk was built in 1688 to replace Holyrood Abbey, which up till then had served as the parish church. The Abbey was commandeered in 1687 by James VII as the chapel for the revived Order of the Thistle. He conveniently ordered that the 'mortification' or bequest of Thomas Moodie should be used to provide the parish with an alternative building, as is recorded on the gable.

The provision of transepts and a chancel, unique in a seventeenth-century Scottish church, raised the suspicion that provision was being made for the reintroduction of Catholicism! The Dutch style of the gable perhaps reflects the fact that the building was completed under James's successor William of Orange, whose arms it bears.

Go into the Canongate Churchyard which has an interesting collection of monuments and fine views across to Calton Hill. Turn left down the side of the church. Doubling back on the grass at the end of the low wall you can find the tomb of Adam Smith, the founder of the science of economics, and guru of the free market, in an enclosure surrounded by railings backing onto the Tollbooth.

Continue down the path along the left side of the church. Up a path to the left is the monument erected by Robert Burns to Robert Fergusson, an Edinburgh poet whom he much admired. Fergusson wrote in Scots and celebrated life in the Old Town in his poem 'Auld Reekie'. He died insane at the age of twenty-three.

Go down the slope, bearing right to reach a green surrounded by enclosed burial plots or lairs. In the middle of the green stands a column commemorating the soldiers who died in the Castle. Surprisingly the Canongate Kirk is the parish church of the Castle as well as of Holyrood Palace.

Return up the other side of the church. Against the wall is the ornate tombstone traditionally supposed to belong to Rizzio, Mary Queen of Scots' Italian secretary and suspected lover. He was murdered before her eyes in Holyrood Palace by a group of lords including her husband Darnley.

Turning left just before reaching the gate, pass the large white statue of a man wrestling with a chimera by Josephine Vasconcellos. It symbolises the triumph of good over evil. A cap badge set in the concrete at its base commemorates its being placed in position by the Royal Engineers. Beyond lies a paved area surrounding the Mercat Cross of the Canongate. Formerly situated in the street outside the Tolbooth, the cross marked the centre of the burgh.

Return to the Canongate and turn left to continue down to **Dunbar's Close**. Turn left into the close. The gate across the bottom is generally unlocked. Passing through, there is a pleasant surprise—a restored seventeenth-century-style formal garden. Paths run between geometric box hedges, and seats in quiet corners suggest a rest. On the right side of the garden stands the eighteenth-century Caddell House.

After a look round leave, ideally by **Panmure Close** at the top left corner of the garden. If it is locked, as it often is, return the way you came in and turn left to reach Panmure Close. The poppies in the ironwork of the gate commemorate Lady Haig's poppy factory which operated here from 1931 until 1965 making the artificial poppies sold on Remembrance Day in aid of wounded servicemen.

Continue down the Canongate and turn left into **Little Lochend Close**, then first right and first left along **Lochend Close**. On your left is Panmure House, a late seventeenth-century mansion where Adam Smith lived from 1778 until his death in 1790, and on your right, a white harled early eighteenth-century house, now the manse of Canongate Kirk.

Turn right into **Lochend Court** which leads to **Buchanan Court** round the side of one of the many new or restored blocks of housing which are rapidly changing the character of this area from industrial to residential. Ahead, the pagoda recalls the days when this area housed breweries and maltings. Across Calton Road, the red sandstone balconied building with brick warehouses behind is the former Craigwell Brewery, converted into flats in 1987.

Turn right along Calton Road and almost immediately right again up **Campbell's Close**. Ahead are the bold concrete tenement stairs designed in 1966 by Basil Spence, Glover and Ferguson as a radical interpretation of the old turrets. Past a Victorian drinking fountain, the close turns right and then left to regain the Canongate.

While a few yards' detour to the right reveals the elegant frontage of the Canongate manse, the walk turns left down the Canongate past Jenny Ha's pub with Jenny the landlady enjoying a pint on the sign.

> A plaque recalls that until 1960 this was Golfer's Land, a tenement reputedly built by a seventeenth century Edinburgh shoemaker, John Paterson, from the proceeds of a golf match. His partner was the Duke of York, the future James VII, who had challenged two English nobles to a round on Leith Links.

To the left is the cul-de-sac of **Brown's Close**. Originally, this was Paterson's Close, then Somerville's Close after a local gunsmith, before finally taking the name of the landowner who was a merchant and Burgess of the city—just one of many examples of close names in the Old Town changing over the centuries.

The building on the left is the eighteenth-century mansion, Whitefoord House, now an ex-servicemen's home incorporating two closes, **Forsyth's Close** and **Galloway's Entry.** On the opposite side of the Canongate, the seventeenth-century Queensberry House is currently being restored as accommodation for the Scottish Parliament with the dramatic new debating chamber to the left.

Queensberry House has had a chequered history as mansion, barracks and old people's home. Ironically, an early owner was William, 2nd Duke of Queensberry, the principal promoter of the Act of Union of 1707 which united the Scottish and English Parliaments at Westminster. It was here that his insane eldest son Lord Drumlanrig was caught roasting a young servant boy on the kitchen spit.

Past the bowling green of Whitefoord House, turn left into **White Horse Close**—perhaps the most picturesque, if not the most authentic close off the Royal Mile. At one time stage coaches for London left from here. Originally an inn called the White Horse, allegedly after Mary Queen of Scots' palfrey which was stabled here, the close was 'restored' and improved in the late nineteenth century as working-class housing. In 1962 it was again restored and let as council housing, although all the flats were subsequently sold to their tenants. The dates appear on the

White Horse Inn

gable at the bottom of the close. Tubs of flowers add to the attractive effect.

Walk through the Close leaving by **Robertson's Close** on the left which twists round onto Calton Road. Turn right past the irregular jumble of buildings of **Robertson's Court** to the roundabout at the foot of the Canongate and opposite the site of the Scottish Parliament. The Parliament, due to open at the end of 2002, is currently enclosed in a hoarding decorated by primary-school class portraits from throughout Scotland.

Walk 5

BREWERS, TEACHERS AND KNIGHTS

Holyrood to St Mary's Street

Starting at Holyrood Palace, the walk takes you up the Canongate and through the 'new town' that is emerging on the site of the Holyroood Brewery alongside the Scottish Parliament. The historic complex around the Palace is followed by dramatic new buildings in the shadow of Arthur's Seat before exploring the new closes around the Scottish Poetry Library.

After visiting the picturesque Bakehouse and Sugarhouse Closes, you go through the grounds of Moray House Institute of Education. Chessel's Court, an early example of 'middle-class' housing in the Old Town, is followed by a descent to Holyrood Road before returning to the Royal Mile at the World's End.

Although this walk is steadily uphill there are no really steep gradients.

Route
Start the walk in Abbey Strand facing the gates of Holyrood Palace, the official residence of the Queen in Scotland.

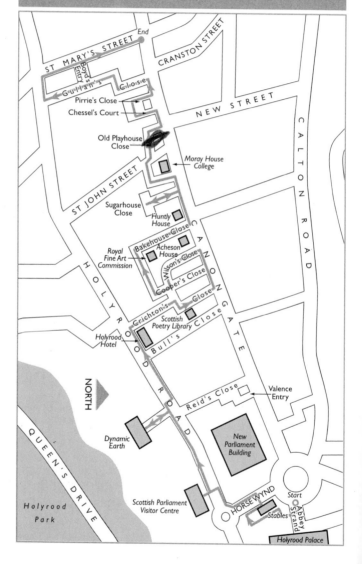

Walk 5 Holyrood to St Mary's Street

ST MARY'S STREET
End
CRANSTON STREET
Boyd's Entry
Gullan's Close
NEW STREET
Pirrie's Close
Chessel's Court
Old Playhouse Close
Moray House College
ST JOHN STREET
Sugarhouse Close
Huntly House
Bakehouse Close
Acheson House
Royal Fine Art Commission
Wilson's Close
Cooper's Close
CALTON ROAD
CANONGATE
Crichton's Close
Scottish Poetry Library
Bull's Close
Holyrood Hotel
NORTH
Valence Entry
Reid's Close
HOLYROOD ROAD
Dynamic Earth
New Parliament Building
QUEEN'S DRIVE
Holyrood Park
Scottish Parliament Visitor Centre
HORSE WYND
Start
Abbey Strand
Stables
Holyrood Palace

The Palace and Abbey are open to the public when not in use for official engagements. On the left is a range of crow-stepped buildings with a covered entrance over a flight of steps dating from the sixteenth century.

The two-storey, eighteenth-century Lucky Spence's house, now housing the Historic Scotland shop, was once a bawdy tavern, later favoured by debtors seeking sanctuary in the Abbey precincts. A path along the side of the shop gives a good view of the recently restored facades of Abbey Strand and leads to Queen Mary's Bath, probably in fact a garden pavilion. On the wall to the right of the Palace gates you will see a large unicorn, the arms of James V of Scotland. It was originally over the gateway to the Palace.

Go through the door on the right into the former stable yard of the Palace. Here you will find the shop and ticket office for the Palace, and a small collection of horse-drawn carriages, including an 1880s omnibus.

Leave by the gate at the far end, passing through a small garden to reach the road. Facing you is an extinct volcano, Arthur's Seat and Salisbury Crags, set in Holyrood Park, a good place for a stroll or a picnic. Edinburgh is unusual in having a mountain in the heart of the city.

Cross the road and turn right past the Scottish Parliament Visitor Centre which has an exhibition of models, drawings and videos illustrating the development of the design of the Parliament Building. Enric Miralles from Barcelona, the lead architect, died in 2000 but construction is continuing to his plans. Although dogged by controversy about its spiralling costs, the Parliament building, which incorporates the seventeenth-century mansion of the Dukes of Queensberry promises to give Scotland's Parliament a fitting new home.

The spiky tented building on your left as you continue along Holyrood Road is Our Dynamic Earth, a Millennium visitor attraction which tells the history of the Planet using the latest entertainment technology. Beyond is the new headquarters of the publishing group whose titles include the *Scotsman* and the *Edinburgh Evening News*.

Cross back over Holyrood Road at the lights and turn left past the luxury hotels and apartments which the presence of the Parliament has attracted. Redevelopment of the former Scottish & Newcastle brewery site is now nearing completion. Its masterplan, launched in the early 1990s, is to emulate, in a modern context, the mix of buildings and uses characteristic of the closes and courts of the Old Town. To achieve an appropriate mix a number of different architects were engaged to design the individual buildings in varying styles and finishes, introducing dramatic reds and dark blues to the more traditional yellows and whites. As it becomes free of construction work, the area with its unexpected corners becomes an intriguing place to wander through.

After the Holyrood Hotel, take the setted lane up the hill past the clock tower, one of the few survivals of the brewery. At the top take the right hand fork, **Crichton's Close**, which runs in front of the new tile-fronted building of the Scottish Poetry Library to emerge on the Canongate beside a striking house. Designed by contemporary Scottish architect Richard Murphy, it continues, in ironwork, the tradition of having an inscription at first floor level.

Turn left along the Canongate passing the head of **Cooper's Close** and the offices of the Old Town Housing Association which, when a community-managed association, was responsible for much of the housing regeneration of the Old Town in the 1980s. Turn left down the stepped **Wilson's Court** which twists its way through modern housing. At the bottom, where steps lead down towards Holyrood Road, turn right and right again up **Bakehouse Close** with the offices of the Royal Fine Art Commission on your right. With its protruding towers and forestairs, Bakehouse Close is one of the most picturesque closes, featuring in many postcards and prints as 'typical' of the Old Town. On the right is the former main entrance to Acheson House.

Doorway of Acheson House

The history of **Acheson House** mirrors that of the Old Town as a whole. Built in 1633 by Sir Archibald Acheson, Secretary of State, it was subsequently subdivided to become a tenement.

In the nineteenth century, it had declined further to become a brothel, known appropriately as the Cock and Trumpet after the Acheson coat of arms above the door. It is amusingly described by Sergeant McLevy in his memoirs, republished as *The Casebook of a Victorian Detective*.

In 1935 it was bought and restored by the Marquis of Bute, and subsequently housed the Scottish Craft Centre for some years. There are plans for it to become an extension to the Museum of Edinburgh.

As you return to the Canongate you pass under the sixteenth-century Huntly House which houses the Museum of Edinburgh. Originally three separate houses, it was never an aristocratic mansion. It takes its name from the Duchess of Gordon of Huntly who had a flat here in the eighteenth century. It is a handsome building with several carved inscriptions on the facade and many fine fireplaces and ceilings inside as well as many relics of Edinburgh's past.

Further up the Canongate look into **Sugarhouse Close**, so named because it was formerly the site of a sugar refinery. It has a very different feel to it from most Old Town closes. Pleasantly whitewashed industrial buildings of the brewery's Technical Department surround a setted court.

A few yards further on is Moray House, dating from about 1625. A prominent, corbelled balcony faces the Canongate. Built for the Countess of Home and taking its name from her daughter, the Countess of Moray, it is now part of the Moray House Institute of Education.

Go past the main gates between the tall pyramids, continuing up the Canongate to the entrance to St John's Street on the left, with a plaque commemorating Godfrey Thomson, the early twentieth-century pioneer of educational testing.

Turn left into St John's Street. On the left, behind a small garden, stands the seventeenth- to eighteenth-century Masonic Lodge, Canongate Kilwinning of the Knights of St John, of which Robert Burns was once a member. At the top of the street, to the left of the pend leading to the Canongate, Tobias Smollett, the author, stayed with his sister on his visit to Edinburgh in 1766.

Just before the pend, turn left into the lane, up steps, and past the headquarters of the masonic Royal Order of Scotland and more college buildings to reach **Old Playhouse Close**. As the name suggests this was the location of the first permanent theatre in Edinburgh between 1747 and 1769.

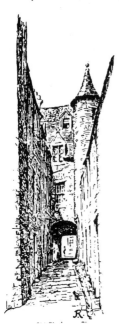

Old Playhouse Close

Turn right to return to the Canongate through the pend. A few yards to the right, down the Canongate, a St John's Cross set in stones in the road marks the site of the cross that indicated the limits of the jurisdiction of the City of Edinburgh. For defensive reasons, the City wished to control the area in front of its gates.

Turn left up the Canongate and then left under the 1960s tenements to reach **Chessel's Court**. Go straight ahead along the path up the side of the large open space, with a green in the middle. Facing you is a handsome white block of mansion flats built in 1748 to meet the pre-New Town demand for middle-class housing. It remains an attractive place to live.

Go round the green to reach **Pirrie's Close**, a pend under the tenements on the Canongate. Turn left to pass the gated entry to **Gibb's Close**.

Turn left into **Gullane Close** which quickly widens into a road bending round via **Boyd's Entry** into St Mary's Street.

Do not follow the road into St Mary's Street but take the continuation of Gullane Close ahead of you down to Holyrood Road, past balconied modern flats. Turn right at the foot to reach the traffic lights.

Diagonally across the junction is the Salvation Army Men's Hostel, formerly one of the Heriot's Trust Schools. It is embellished by seventeenth-century style carvings derived from Heriot's Hospital (see Walk 10). To the left of the Hostel you can see one of the remaining stretches of the Flodden Wall, which originally ran right around this side of the city.

Turn right up St Mary's Street. It follows the line of St Mary's Wynd which ran just outside the east wall of the city. The street was widened in 1869 as one of the first developments under the 1867 Improvement Act. The east side was rebuilt as Victorian baronial tenements with shops underneath which still make handsome housing. The 1970s office block on the west side, now a hotel, is less attractive.

St Mary's Street contains some interesting shops selling everything from wood-burning stoves to high fashion. Note the Art Deco front on Casey's sweet shop and the carved bull's head on the corner of Boyd's Entry. At the traffic lights you regain the Royal Mile, and reach the end of the walk.

Walk 6

ROBBERS, SKINNERS AND PAUPERS

St Mary's Street to South Bridge

This walk draws together many of the building periods of the Old Town, each with its distinctive style and purpose. It also passes two of the city's more unusual attractions, the Museum of Childhood and St Cecilia's Hall, with its unique collection of old musical instruments. You should have time to stop off at places of interest as the walk is short with little serious climbing.

The walk twists and turns through the closes and pends between the High Street and the Cowgate, once a desirable address, now the haunt of students and clubbers. The old houses of Tweeddale Court and Skinner's Close contrast sharply with the pastiche 'Old Town' of the Crowne Plaza Hotel. You also pass the scene of two unsolved crimes.

Route

The walk starts outside the World's End pub at the crossing of the Royal Mile with St Mary's Street. *Trompe l'œil* paintings on the pub give a dramatic interpretation of the name

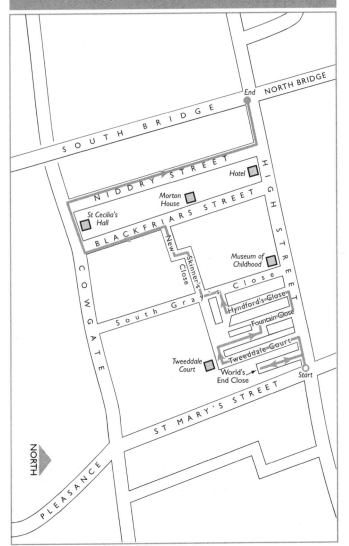

NORTH BRIDGE

End

SOUTH BRIDGE

NIDDRY STREET

Hotel

HIGH STREET

Morton House

BLACKFRIARS STREET

St Cecilia's Hall

New Close

Skinner's Close

Museum of Childhood

Close

South Gray's Close

Hyndford's Close

Fountain Close

COWGATE

Tweeddale Court

Tweeddale Court

World's End Close

Start

ST MARY'S STREET

NORTH

PLEASANCE

which merely indicates the end of the historic City of Edinburgh. It was from this pub that over twenty years ago two girls set out on their last and tragic journey. Their murder remains unsolved to this day.

Go up the High Street and turn left into **World's End Close** with its small garden enclosed by the backs of tenements.

Return to the High Street, turn left and then left again through the decorative green archway with its elaborate crest into **Tweeddale Court**.

On the right of the close stands an inconspicuous shed which, it is claimed, was once a sedan chair store. Sedan chairs were enclosed chairs on poles carried by two men. They were used by the gentry in the sev-

Tweeddale Court

enteenth and eighteenth centuries to move around the closes without getting their finery filthy.

At the bottom of the close stands Tweeddale House.

Tweeddale House was built about 1600, and in 1670 became the town house of the Marquess of Tweeddale. By

1750 it was in a ruinous state. It was repaired and extended by John and Robert Adam to become the headquarters of the British Linen Bank.

The bank was the scene of one of Edinburgh's classic crimes when in November 1806 William Begbie, the bank's messenger, was neatly stabbed and robbed of £4,000. Though £3,000 was subsequently found in a hole in a wall in a garden near Leith, the murderer was never caught.

After the Bank moved to St Andrew Square in the New Town, the house was taken over by Oliver & Boyd, publishers and printers of the textbooks used by generations of Scottish school children and exported throughout the world. Their name is still above the door and a hoist for lifting paper can be seen on the adjacent house.

Next door is the headquarters of the Saltire Society, which promotes all aspects of Scottish culture and presents awards for buildings of architectural merit.

Double back behind the sedan chair store, turning left and right to reach the High Street via **Fountain Close**. This close and the adjacent Hyndford Close were reinstated within a largely new sheltered housing scheme built in 1986. It shows how closes can be used in a traditional way to provide quiet, covered access.

Turn left up the High Street and left again into **Hyndford Close**. Take the first right to reach **South Gray's Close**, arriving underneath a glazed overpass. The overpass is part of the Museum of Childhood, whose entrance is on the High Street at the top of the close. It houses a large collection of toys and other paraphernalia of childhood from earliest times to the present day. Very popular with children, it also provides grown-ups of all ages with the opportunity for nostalgic reminiscence.

Turn left down South Gray's Close. Ahead on the left stands St Patrick's Church, a handsome classical building built in 1772 for an Episcopal congregation and now the main Roman Catholic church in the Old Town.

Take the first turning to the right into a narrow road, **New Skinner's Close**. The house on the left with the hexagonal turret was built in 1643 as the Skinner's Hall, the headquarters of the Incorporation of Skinners. It later housed the Edinburgh Industrial School founded by Dr Guthrie in 1847 to give poor children a practical and Christian education.

On the left at the bend **Coynie House Close** commemorates the location of the Mint. The gate to the close leading to the back areas of restored houses is often locked.

Continue along New Skinner's Close to reach Blackfriars Street.

> **Blackfriars Street** was known as Blackfriars Wynd until widened under the 1867 Improvement Act. It was perhaps selected for treatment because of the notoriety it had gained through the publication in 1850 of the pamphlet *Blackfriars' Wynd Analyzed* by George Bell MD.
>
> His survey estimated that at that time the 142 dwellings in the Wynd housed 1,025 inhabitants, about a third of whom were children under 14. He calculated that each inhabitant had a mere 188 cubic feet of living space comparing this with the 800 cubic feet of a prison cell!
>
> Yet Bell selected the Wynd as being average rather than particularly bad! He states explicitly that the closes

off the Grassmarket, and Todrick's Wynd, demolished when Blackfriars Wynd was widened, were worse.

Doorway of Morton House

Turn left into Blackfriars Street. This side of the road dates from the widening, and the section nearest the High Street has recently been extensively renovated. On the other side, near the top, Morton House, built in the sixteenth and seventeenth centuries, is now a youth hostel. Further down on the right is the car park of the Crowne Plaza Hotel.

Go down to the Cowgate. On the left at the corner a former school houses St Anne's Community Centre, a facility serving the whole of the Old Town. On the Cowgate side of the building a stone plaque records the site of Cardinal Beaton's palace: the Cowgate, facing south, was historically a good address.

Turn right along the Cowgate. On your right, a modern frontage conceals St Cecilia's Concert Hall, built in 1761 for the Musical Society of Edinburgh and still in use as a concert hall under the management of Edinburgh University. It also houses a famous collection of old musical instruments which can be visited on Wednesday and Saturday afternoons. On the opposite side of the Cowgate is one of several recently built blocks of student housing. Ahead the South Bridge spans the Cowgate.

Turn right into the narrow canyon of Niddry Street, its tenements which front on to South Bridge now largely restored following decades of dereliction.

Towards the High Street on the right is the Crowne Plaza Hotel. Built in 1988 using ultra-modern techniques, it tries to look old, even retaining the close names for some of its entrances. In the view of many it succeeds, and it is certainly a great improvement on some of the earlier large-scale developments in the Old Town. The horizontal storeys, which do not follow the fall of the street, however, give the game away.

On reaching the High Street turn left across the front of the Bank Hotel to reach South Bridge and the end of the walk.

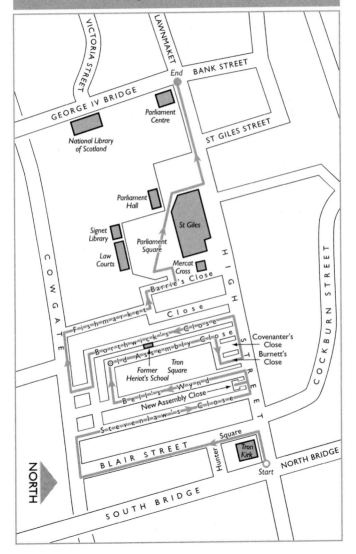

Walk 7 South Bridge to George IV Bridge

VICTORIA STREET

LAWNMAKET

End

BANK STREET

GEORGE IV BRIDGE

Parliament Centre

National Library of Scotland

ST GILES STREET

Parliament Hall

St Giles

Signet Library

Parliament Square

HIGH

Law Courts

Mercat Cross

Barrie's Close

C O W G A T E

Close

F=i=s=h=m=a=r=k=e=t

C=l=o=s=e

B=o=r=t=h=w=i=c=k='=s

C=l=o=s=e

O=l=d A=s=s=e=m=b=l=y C=l=o=s=e

Former Heriot's School

Tron Square

Covenanter's Close

Burnett's Close

HIGH STREET

B=e=l=l='=s W=y=n=d

New Assembly Close

S=t=e=v=e=n=l=a=w='=s C=l=o=s=e

BLAIR STREET

Hunter Square

Tron Kirk

Start

NORTH BRIDGE

SOUTH BRIDGE

COCKBURN STREET

NORTH

Walk 7

JUDGES, PRISONERS AND REFORMERS

South Bridge to George IV Bridge

This walk weaves its way in and out of the closes running down from the High Street to the Cowgate, ending at the point where Law, Church and State meet. It involves a few stiff climbs through some of the longest closes in the Old Town.

After descending by Blair Street and returning by Stevenlaw's Close you pass New Assembly Close, the meeting place of Edinburgh society in the eighteenth century. Passing through Tron Square, an early council housing development rather out of character with the Old Town, you regain the High Street via Old Assembly Close, and an optional detour to two additional closes for those who wish to collect as many as possible!

The atmospheric Borthwick's Close heads down to the Cowgate. Returning via Fleshmarket Close and the tiny Barrie's Close, you pop up again in the very heart of the City, Parliament Close. Here, you will find the Mercat Cross, the High Courts, Parliament Hall, the High Kirk of St Giles and the obscure grave of a national leader.

Route

The walk starts on the corner of South Bridge, outside the Tron Church.

South Bridge was built in 1785 to give convenient access to Edinburgh from the South. Alhough only one arch is visible in the Cowgate, the street is carried on a total of nineteen arches. Unfortunately, Robert Adam's monumental design for the buildings lining the bridge was not adopted. South Bridge was a rather down-market shopping street until a recent comprehensive renovation scheme, which has restored the stonework and re-introduced traditional shop fronts.

> The **Tron Kirk** was built in 1636-47 to house one of the congregations displaced when St Giles was briefly appropriated as a cathedral during a royal attempt to introduce bishops to Scotland. The spire of the Tron was damaged in the great fire of 1824 which destroyed the whole area from here to Parliament Close. It was rebuilt four years later.
>
> Inside, the foundations of another close, **Marlin's Wynd**, demolished when the Tron was built, are preserved. For some years used as an Old Town Information Centre each summer, its future is uncertain.

Turn left into Hunter Square, the open space surrounding the Tron. Recently pedestrianised and refurbished, this square contains modern sculptures by Ian Hamilton Finlay and Peter Randall Page, granite benches and useful public conveniences. Here, too, as well as at the Mercat Cross, you will find boards advertising a wide range of guided walks round the Old Town, several featuring ghosts and other horrors!

Continue down Blair Street, largely rehabilitated but with some buildings still in poor repair. Both Blair Street and Hunter Square are named after James Hunter Blair, Provost from 1784-86 and one of the chief promoters of South Bridge. There are benefits in having a double-barrelled name!

Turn right into the Cowgate and right again at the next opening. The steep, well-paved and step-free slope of **Stevenlaw's Close** leads back up to the High Street. Originally many more of the closes were simply slopes. This permitted barrows to be wheeled up and down, but must have been dangerous in frosty weather!

Turn left into the High Street. The next close, **New Assembly Close**, housed from 1766-84 the city's Assembly Rooms, where society gathered for balls and receptions. The classical house at its foot was built as the Commercial Bank in 1813, a date when the choice of a New Town site might have been expected.

Continue a few yards up the High Street to **Bell's Wynd**, which descends steeply down past Tron Square, an early attempt at slum clearance by the City Council in 1899. Take the flight of steps up on the right about 15 yards before the bend in the close, leading to the large drying green between the two main blocks of Tron Square, and cut across to the foot of **Old Assembly Close**.

Turn up Old Assembly Close, the site of the Assembly Rooms from 1720 to 1766. The building on the left-hand side was one of the charitable schools set up by the

Heriot's Trust in 1839 to give poor children of the Old Town a basic education. Note the inscription above the door and the elegant cupola. Latterly a wire works, the building is now used by the Faculty of Advocates. On the right of the close, two wide terraces with seats offer the chance of a rest, watched over by a colony of very well-fed cats.

To cover the maximum possible number of closes, turn right into the yard just behind the High Street frontage and pass **Covenanter's Close** to reach the High Street by **Burnett's Close**. These closes have little to commend them, being essentially the back yards and rubbish stores of the High Street pubs. Alternatively, carry on up Old Assembly Close to the High Street entrance where the faded paintwork of the wire works sign can still be seen on either side.

On regaining the High Street turn left past the Festival Fringe Offices, decorated with brightly painted figures. Turn left down **Borthwick's Close**, an atmospheric, dark entry with just a slit of light visible. At the foot, the close turns into a setted road which bends left. Take the first right after the bend to reach the Cowgate beside the Siglio, a leisure pub. As well as student residences, the Cowgate is notable for its concentration of clubs and discos.

Turn right and re-ascend by **Fishmarket Close**, a setted road leading to a car park. The building on the right was at one time the Edinburgh Sabbath Free Breakfast Mission, ministering to the physical and spiritual hunger of local paupers at one sitting. Continue upwards until the road bends to the right. A gated entry to the left, **Barrie's Close**, is worth taking if it is open.

At first very unpromising, Barrie's Close turns to the right to reveal a steep flight of steps leading up into Parliament Close. If the gate is shut, continue up Fishmarket Close and turn left to reach Parliament Close.

Parliament Close or Square, the area surrounding the High Kirk of St Giles, was once the centre of government in Scotland. At its entrance stands the Mercat Cross, reconstructed in 1885 at the expense of William Gladstone, Prime Minister and local MP. Note the sprightly unicorn on the top of the central column. Proclamations of elections or of the ascent of a new monarch to the throne are still made from the Mercat Cross three days after they are made in London, to allow for the time the messenger would have taken to reach here on horseback!

The Mercat Cross

Following the arcade round, look for the Royal Arms over the door marked Exchequer. On the south side of the Kirk stands a lead equestrian statue of Charles II in a Roman toga, probably imported from Holland. Also in this area, which was originally part of the churchyard of St Giles, is the grave of John Knox, founder of the Church of Scotland. You may be able to spot an inconspicuous yellow square marking the spot in the car parking space 44, assuming that there is not a car obscuring it. It is a rather humble memorial to a man who had such an influence on Scotland's destiny.

Parliament Close or Square is the hub of justice in Scotland, which retains its own distinctive legal system. The Square houses a number of courts including the Court of Session, the ultimate recourse of appeal. It also contains the Signet and Advocates' libraries and the seventeenth-century Parliament House where the Scottish Parliament met until the Union of 1707.

You can visit Parliament Hall with its magnificent hammer-beam roof. If the courts are in session, you may be able to explore behind their imposing facades or to see the advocates, the Scottish equivalent of barristers, scurrying across the Square in their black gowns and wigs.

St Giles

Go along the south side of St Giles or under the arcades of the Law Courts. The square now widens out again in front of the west end of St Giles. In the centre is an ornate statue of 1888, decorated with bronze stags, to the Duke of Buccleuch, possibly the richest land-owner in Scotland.

Close to it brass markers outline the site of the Tolbooth Prison. It was immortalised by Sir Walter Scott as *The Heart of Midlothian* in his novel of that title. The site of the prison is also marked by a heart set out in the cobbles, on which it is traditional to spit for luck—a tradition still commonly upheld!

Turn left past another well and the neo-classical Parliament Offices, built in 1900-5. On the balustrade, there is a detailed description of the buildings of Parliament Square. The traffic lights at George IV Bridge mark the end of this walk.

Walk 8

Burgher, Mason and Burglar

George IV Bridge to the Castle

This walk takes you to attractive closes associated with two notable Edinburgh characters. Brodie's Close is named after the family home of Deacon Brodie, a respectable city councillor by day and burglar by night, while in Riddle's Court Baillie Macmorran entertained the King, before his untimely end as a victim of classroom violence!

A stroll along sunny Victoria Terrace, with spectacular views over the Grassmarket, takes you to Johnston Terrace and on to Castlehill where you can visit two closes on the way back to the Castle Esplanade. This marks the end of the walk and, if you have been doing all the walks in order, your exploration of the closes of the Royal Mile.

Route

Start at the corner of George IV Bridge and the Lawnmarket, outside the Scottish Parliament administration offices built for Midlothian County Council in 1968, at a time when architecture made no attempt to fit in with its surroundings. It is the most out-of-place building in the Royal Mile.

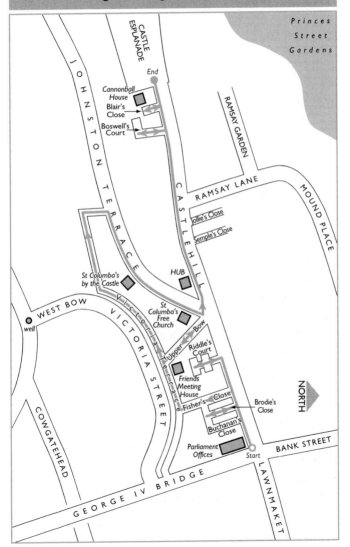

Walk 8 George IV Bridge to The Castle

Princes Street Gardens

CASTLE ESPLANADE

JOHNSTON TERRACE

End

Cannonball House

Blair's Close

Boswell's Court

RAMSAY GARDEN

RAMSAY LANE

CASTLE HILL

MOUND PLACE

Jollie's Close

Semple's Close

HUB

St Columba's by the Castle

St Columba's Free Church

Upper Bow

Riddle's Court

WEST BOW

well

VICTORIA STREET

Victoria Terrace

Friends Meeting House

Fisher's Close

Brodie's Close

Buchanan's Close

COWGATEHEAD

Parliament Offices

Start

BANK STREET

LAWNMARKET

NORTH

GEORGE IV BRIDGE

Moving on up the Lawnmarket, past the blue police box, you pass the gated **Buchanan's Close**. Turn left into **Brodie's Close**, named after the family of the notorious Deacon Brodie.

> The son of a prosperous cabinetmaker, **Deacon William Brodie** rose to the top position in the Wrights and Masons of Edinburgh, one of the city's craft guilds. In 1781 he was elected to the City Council.
>
> Unbeknown to his respectable colleagues he was also an inveterate gambler and lover of the low life of the city, frequenting the drinking dens and cock-fighting pits of the Grassmarket. About 1786 his legitimate earnings became insufficient to support his debauches and he set himself up as the leader of a gang of burglars. He carried out several daring robberies using his position to get access to keys, which he then copied.
>
> When a robbery of the Excise Office in Chessel's Court went wrong, one of his accomplices, attracted by the offer of a free pardon, 'shopped' him. Brodie was pursued to Amsterdam, arrested, brought back to Edinburgh, convicted and hanged in 1788.
>
> The story that he was the first person to be hanged on a new type of scaffold designed by himself does not stand up to scrutiny. His casual and humorous deportment on the scaffold gave rise to the story that he had devised a way of cheating the gallows, but if so it failed. Deacon Brodie was Stevenson's model for his novel *Dr Jekyll and Mr Hyde*.

The Brodies' house was entered by the handsome door in a turnpike stair on the right. It is now a Masonic Hall, the home of the Celtic Lodge, founded in 1821 to promote the wearing of Highland dress.

As the gate at the end of the close is locked, return to the Lawnmarket and turn left, past Fisher's Close, to which you will return. Turn left into **Riddle's Court**, its picturesque courtyards linked by a passageway .

In the first court David Hume lived before moving to more spacious premises in James' Court (see Walk 1). Note the external wooden stair, once a feature of the Old Town closes. In the second court is the house built about 1592 by Baillie Macmorran, now used by the Workers' Educational Association.

Baillie Macmorran's house

Reputedly the richest merchant in Edinburgh, **Baillie John Macmorran** entertained James VI and his queen, Anne of Denmark, to a grand banquet in his house in 1593.

In 1595 he suffered the remarkable fate of being shot dead while trying to quell a schoolboy riot in the High School, then in High School Yards. Protesting at not being granted an expected holiday, the pupils had barricaded themselves in the school. Baillie Macmorran was directing the city officers in breaking through the barricades when he was shot in the head by William Sinclair, son of the Chancellor of Caithness.

Although the Macmorran family pressed for justice, the culprit's aristocratic connections prevailed on the King to release him after a short spell in prison. Clearly some progress has been made in school discipline!

Return to the Lawnmarket, turn right and then right again into **Fisher's Close**, a long passage with some widenings which gives a good impression of the enclosure of the closes.

Go down the close and turn right onto **Victoria Terrace**, built in 1829-34 with Victoria Street and Johnston Terrace to provide convenient access to the city from the west. The Terrace runs across the roofs of the shops in Victoria Street below, providing good views.

Along the Terrace there is a fine array of former churches of various denominations, attracted perhaps by the desire to 'fly the flag' on the doorstep of the Church of Scotland's Assembly Halls. Baden-Powell House at the end of the close, built in 1865 as a Primitive Methodist Chapel is followed by Kirk House, built over an arcade as an Original Secession chapel, also in 1865, and now used by the Quakers.

Across Victoria Street, the former St John's Church of 1840 is a pub, while on Upper Bow, St Columba's Free Church is still used by the Free Church of Scotland.

Upper Bow, a short street which now appears to be a dead end, joins the Terrace from the right, its former route marked by a flight of steps going down to the top of the West Bow, the continuation of Victoria Street. This steep passage zig-zagging up the side of the ridge used to be the main way into the city from the West. At the top of Upper Bow stood the Weighhouse or Butter Tron where butter and cheese were sold.

Continue along Victoria Terrace, with fine view across

the Grassmarket to Greyfriars Churchyard and the seventeenth-century Heriot's Hospital, now a school. At the foot of the West Bow stands the Bow Well, one of the city's oldest, dating from 1674. On the right side of the West Bow there are some fine seventeenth-century tenements.

Victoria Terrace now becomes a close. Continue along and up the steps to Johnston Terrace, passing the offices of the Scottish Genealogical Society on the right. On the corner is yet another church—St Columba's by the Castle— this time Episcopalian. The Castle is now in full view. Johnston Terrace was the solution finally adopted in 1827 to give access to the city from the west; other suggestions included a viaduct the length of the Grassmarket!

Turn right along Johnston Terrace and cross at the roundabout. Turn left up Castlehill, past the imposing Highland Tolbooth Church.

Built in 1839-44 as the Assembly Hall of the Church of Scotland, the **Highland Tolbooth Church** was designed by James Gillespie Graham with help from A W N Pugin, the leading proponent of Gothic architecture. Pugin happened to be in Edinburgh, having been shipwrecked and brought ashore at Leith. The church has been imaginatively converted into **The Hub**, the headquarters of the Edinburgh International Festival Society, with ticket sales, a café and performance spaces.

Going up Castlehill you can see on the opposite side the gated **Jollie's** and **Semple's Closes**.

Turn left into **Boswell's Close** to admire the leafy

courtyard of the Witchery by the Castle restaurant. A plaque commemorates the meeting of Dr Johnson with his biographer James Boswell.

Returning to Castlehill, continue past the Scotch Whisky Heritage Centre, where you can take a ride in a barrel through a history of Scotch, to Cannonball House.

The sixteenth-century Cannonball House takes its name from the 'cannonball' embedded in its gable. Despite stories of dramatic sieges, this is more prosaically a marker showing the level of the supply from which the reservoir opposite received its water. The house is now the Education Centre for the Parliament.

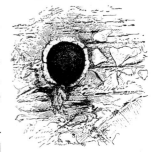

Cannonball House

The gate just before Cannonball House leads to the unlabelled **Blair's Close** and the back of Cannonball House and the Whisky Heritage Centre. Unfortunately the other exits from the close are locked.

The walk finishes on the Castle Esplanade at the top of Castlehill with fine views to the north over the New Town to Fife, to the South over the Grassmarket to the Pentland Hills, and lastly down the Royal Mile, back into the Old Town.

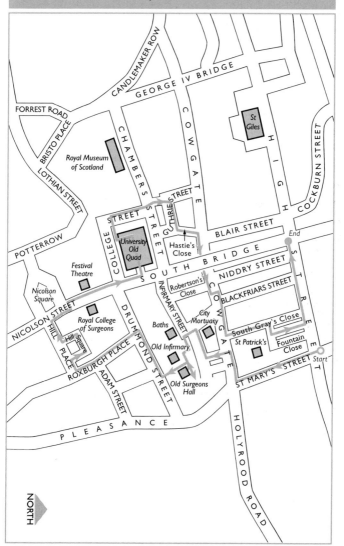

Walk 9

Surgeons, Students and Physicians

The University Quarter

This walk explores some of the sites associated with the individuals and institutions which have given the city its international reputation for medicine and scholarship. It takes in the classical grandeur of the Old College of Edinburgh University and the Royal College of Surgeons, as well as some rather more off-beat sights, from a Victorian baths to the City Mortuary.

The route lies to the south of the Old Town and includes some of the streets built just before the radical solution of building a New Town to the north of the city was adopted. Many of Edinburgh's institutions grew up in this area, including its University, hospital and one of its first schools. All have long since expanded into other parts of the city but some of the original buildings can still be seen.

The one drawback to this walk is that some areas of the University may be closed on Sundays, especially during the vacations.

Route

The walk starts outside the World's End pub, where St Mary's Street meets the Royal Mile. Turn down St Mary's Street where in the fourtenth century there was a convent and hospital run by Cistercian nuns. By the mid-nineteenth century St Mary's Wynd had become a notorious slum and one of the first works under the 1867 Improvement Act was to widen the street and replace the slums with Scots Baronial tenements.

Cross the Cowgate at the traffic lights at the bottom of St Mary's Street and turn right along the Cowgate. The first building that you pass is the Salvation Army Men's Hostel, built in 1840 as a school by the Heriot's Trust. There are several hostels for the homeless in the Old Town, some of which date back to the nineteenth century. They were built to cope with the arrival of poor immigrants with no home or money and few prospects.

Take the second flight of steps on the left up the side of the modern City Mortuary to High School Yards. Here Edinburgh City Council built tenements in the early twentieth century to replace some of the Old Town slums. Note the balconies designed to give residents access to fresh air at a time when TB was a major scourge.

Turn right at the top of the stairs past the mortuary and then left into Infirmary Street. Diagonally opposite and slightly to the right are the Victorian, Venetian-style, Infirmary Street Baths, now unfortunately closed. Their future is very uncertain after developing a serious leak. These public baths were essential at a time when many houses

Lady Yester's Church

did not have access to a bath or a place to wash clothes. They were erected on the site of a rather more fashionable spa bath, which King George IV may have patronised on his visit to Edinburgh in 1822.

The building on the corner immediately across from you is the former Lady Yester's Church. It was once the most popular church with medical students, as they could hear the bell signalling the start of an operation from their pew.

Go through the gate on your left, opening into a court-yard fronting the former High School building, now part of the University.

The High School was built in 1777 to replace an earlier and smaller building nearer the Cowgate. Its pupils included Walter Scott and Lord Brougham, after whom the carriage was named. In 1829, the school moved across the valley to Calton Hill and in the 1960s moved again to a site on the outskirts of the city.

After the school moved, the building became a surgical hospital. The pioneers of modern surgery, James Syme and Joseph Lister, both had wards here. After a period as a fever hospital, the building now houses experts whose interest in bones is very different, in the Centre for Field Archaeology.

The University buildings on the right incorporate traces of the hospital building designed by William Adam in the 1740s. Most of the hospital was rebuilt in the mid-nineteenth century to meet the demands of a vastly increased population and more modern medical practice. The new building, in turn, was soon found to be inadequate for its purpose and the Infirmary moved once more to its present site in Lauriston Place in 1873. It is about to move again to the southern outskirts of the city. (See Walk 10 for this and one or two other medical locations.)

Cross the courtyard diagonally, bearing slightly to the right. As you go through the arch under the buildings into Surgeons Square, look back to a dramatic view of the chimneys of the hospital and Infirmary Street Baths. On the right side of the square stands the former Surgeons Hall, built in 1697 as a meeting place for the profession. Another building in the Square at one time housed the anatomy classes for which the infamous Burke and Hare provided the bodies.

Take the ramp running between the buildings half way down the square on the right, and climb the stairs to the car park at the top. Turn to the right to reach the gate and going through it turn right into Drummond Street. The elaborate gateposts at the entrance of the former hospital were designed by Adam.

Drummond Street follows the line of 'Thief Raw' which ran outside the Flodden Wall, a section of which can still be seen. Look along Drummond Street and on the left you can find a reminder of the origins of the surgeon's skill. The red and white stripes of the barber's pole recall the historic association of that trade with the more bloody one of surgeon.

Take the second road on the left, Roxburgh Place, opposite Drummond Street School, now converted into housing. Before turning the corner look ahead for one of the best views of the dome of Edinburgh University.

In Roxburgh Place a Georgian tenement is followed by some of the brutal concrete buildings of the 1960s' expansion of the University, which destroyed much of the inner south side of the city. On the right is the Department of Anatomy, on the left, after Lady Glenorchy's Church and Hall, the Institute of Occupational Medicine.

At the next street to the left, Roxburgh Street becomes Richmond Place. Turn right into Hill Place to reach Hill Square.

Hill Square is a New Town Square in miniature, built by James Hill in 1809. It is largely occupied by medical institutions and firms as indicated by the numerous brass plates. The former church on the east side of the square was converted into a medical symposium hall in the early 1980s through the generosity of the King of Saudi Arabia.

The discreet entrance to the museum of the Royal College of Surgeons can be found on the north side of the square. It contains a fascinating collection of medical memorabilia including a purse made from the skin of Burke, the murderer and bodysnatcher, and one of the world's largest collections of dentists' chairs.

Continue up Hill Place past the neat little Post Office

on the corner, and turn right into Nicolson Street, the southern extension of South Bridge. Opposite lies Nicolson Square, built in 1765. In the gardens in the middle of the square is the statue of a brass-founder, designed for the Edinburgh International Exhibition of 1886.

Old College

Cross the road at the lights and continue up Nicolson Street passing the new Festival Theatre with its dramatic glass frontage and, almost opposite, the grand pillared frontage of Surgeons Hall, built in 1829 by William Playfair to replace the altogether more modest premises you saw earlier.

Carry on across College Street and turn left through the monumental portals of Edinburgh University's Old College, designed by Robert Adam in 1789, as is indicated over the entrance. The interior of the College was completed by William Playfair after a halt to building during the Napoleonic Wars. Playfair substituted one large rectangular quadrangle for the two originally proposed by Adam. It is a pity that this magnificent space is used as a car park.

Old College was the home of the University Medical School until the 1880s. Some of the more unusual students included Dr Paul Roget, more famous to posterity for his thesaurus, and Charles Darwin, who left after a year because he could not stand the sight of blood.

There is a legend that a tunnel runs from the former Anatomy Department in Old College to the Cowgate. It was used for the delivery of cadavers by the body snatchers or Resurrectionists, as their activities would be less likely to attract attention in the general squalor of the Cowgate.

When the University is open, it is possible to reach West College Street through a corridor outside the Talbot Rice Art Gallery in the left corner opposite the entrance of the College. If this is not possible, return to College Street and take the first right. Go down West College Street, under the 'Bridge of Sighs', to Chambers Street.

Chambers Street, linking George IV and South Bridges, was the largest single development resulting from the 1867 Improvement Act. On the left is the Royal Museum of Scotland with its magnificent glass and iron entrance hall, and beyond, the new Museum of Scotland. Opposite, the former Heriot-Watt University facade now fronts a new Sheriff Court Building.

Cross Chambers Street and go down the steps to Guthrie Street, which snakes down to the Cowgate. Cross the road, and turn right past the front of the new tenements built to replace those destroyed by a gas explosion in 1990. Take **Hastie's Close** to the left on the corner, noting the fine juxtaposition of street lighting.

The close dog-legs round Wilkie House, formerly the Cowgate Free Church and now a club venue.

At the foot of the close, turn right into the Cowgate which takes you under South Bridge. This is the heart of Edinburgh's club scene. Cross **Robertson's Close**, which despite its name is navigable by car; in this close was Edinburgh's original infirmary with six beds.

Cross the Cowgate at the pedestrian crossing and go along the side of St Ann's Community Centre, housed in a former school on the site of a Cardinal's palace. Turn left up **South Gray's Close** past the entrance to the eighteenth-century St Patrick's Church. Turn right into **Fountain Court** and at the end of the sheltered housing on the left, just before the wall, turn left into **Fountain Close**, going up the short flight of steps. To the dispensary for the poor that was once housed in this close can be traced the origin of the Royal College of Physicians of Edinburgh.

Turn left and you are now back on the familiar territory of the High Street. One of the dummy closes incorporated in the Crowne Plaza Hotel on your left as you walk up to the traffic lights is one last reminder of Edinburgh's medical past. **Dickson's Close** was the site of the original Surgeons Hall before it moved to the two buildings that you have already visited on this walk.

Walk 10

MAGGIE DICKSON, GREYFRIARS BOBBY AND JINGLING GEORDIE

The Old Town South of the Castle

This walk explores the historic area to the South of Edinburgh Castle. En route, you can see traces of the three stages of the city's fortifications and view the Castle from some unusual angles. Historic sights along the way include the Grassmarket, scene of fairs, riots and hangings, the Magdalen Chapel, Greyfriars Churchyard with its Covenanters' prison, and Heriot's Hospital.

This walk also brings together many of the features of the other walks round the Old Town—unexpected views, wells, memorials to the famous and the infamous and, of course, some more closes. It is one of the longer walks, especially if you explore Greyfriars Churchyard, but there are plenty of cafes, pubs and take-aways to sustain you on your way.

Route

Start at the corner of the Lawnmarket and George IV

Walk 10 The Old Town South of the Castle

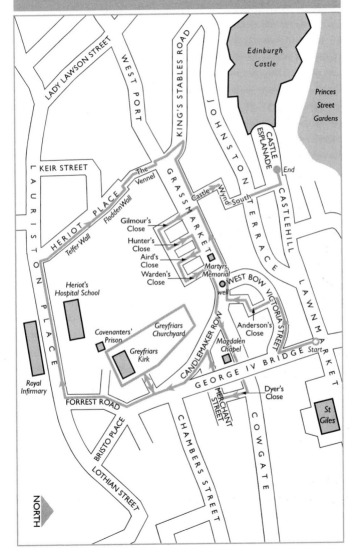

Edinburgh Castle

Princes Street Gardens

LADY LAWSON STREET

WEST PORT

KING'S STABLES ROAD

JOHNSTON

CASTLE ESPLANADE

End

CASTLEHILL

KEIR STREET

LAURISTON PLACE

HERIOT PLACE

The Vennel

Flodden Wall

Telfer Wall

GRASSMARKET

Castle Wynd South

TERRACE

LAWNMARKET

Gilmour's Close

Hunter's Close

Aird's Close

Warden's Close

Martyrs' Memorial

WEST BOW

well

VICTORIA STREET

Heriot's Hospital School

Covenanters' Prison

Greyfriars Churchyard

Greyfriars Kirk

CANDLEMAKER ROW

Anderson's Close

Magdalen Chapel

GEORGE IV BRIDGE

Start

Royal Infirmary

FORREST ROAD

MERCHANT STREET

Dyer's Close

MARKET

St Giles

BRISTO PLACE

CHAMBERS STREET

COWGATE

LOTHIAN STREET

NORTH

Bridge. Go along the latter, past the uninspired concrete block built as Council offices to replace the Victorian Royal Medical Society where many eminent nineteenth-century medics delivered their first scientific paper. It now houses the administration of the Scottish Parliament.

Cross Victoria Street and head down its canyon-like curve. The street was created in the early nineteenth century to give better access into the city from the west. As you descend you may see a wedding party posing for the camera outside the Registry Office. A few doors along is the former St John's Church, now converted into an entertainment complex.

Turn left into **Anderson's Close**. This dark and slightly sinister close leads you down by two right angles into Cowgatehead between the Grassmarket Advice Centre and the Greyfriars Hotel, a hostel for the homeless. The contrast with the upmarket shops of Victoria Street is striking. Turn right into the open expanse of the Grassmarket.

In the Middle Ages the **Grassmarket** was the city's trading quarter. Fairs were held long before the charter granted by James III for a cattle fair in 1477. It later became a horse and timber market and goods transit depot. Here carts and carriages were unloaded and the goods carried up the steep incline of the West Bow by barrow or porter.

Round it grew up the inns and stables used by the carters; traditionally the stable was paid for, the carter sleeping in the loft free! In the yards behind, cow feeders fattened up cattle before they made their final journey to the meat market, where the College of Art now stands.

Always a raffish area with many drinking dens, in the nineteenth century the Grassmarket became one of the city's most notorious slums. The carters' quarters turned into hostels for the homeless: as late as the 1970s there were four in the area. Although the pubs remain, the Grassmarket is now a popular place to live.

Cross the foot of the West Bow to the 'island', noting as you pass the well, the blue former Police Box and the red, traditional-style phone box. Turn right and then left along the island to reach the walled area of the Covenanters' Memorial.

The **Covenanters** took their name from the National Covenant, signed in Greyfriars Churchyard in 1638 to protest against King Charles I's attempt to introduce bishops to the Church of Scotland. Siding with Parliament during the Civil War, the Covenanters were hunted down after Charles II regained the throne.

Between 1680-88, about 100 Covenanters of all ages and both sexes were hanged or, as a cynical judge put it, sent to 'Glorify God in the Grassmarket'. A steel plaque on the wall records their names. The monument is still the destination of street marches by the Scottish Orange Order.

The Grassmarket was for many years the site of public hangings. This is commemorated in the names of two local pubs. The Last Drop is obvious but less so is Maggie Dickson's. Maggie was hung in the Grassmarket but as her grieving relatives carted her body away for burial, she suddenly sat bolt upright. This earned her the nickname 'half-hangit Maggie'. She lived to a ripe old age.

Cross the busy road at the pedestrian crossing and turn right for a few yards. For those wishing to see as many closes as possible, there are four more which connect to the yard behind. This yard has had a varied history. At one time it was the Castle Brewery, one of several such establishments benefiting from the multitude of fresh water springs in the area. It then became the College of Mines, and thereafter part of Heriot-Watt University; it is currently part of Edinburgh College of Art.

Go right to the top of **Gilmour's Close**, before turning left, and left again to return to the Grassmarket by **Hunter's Close**. The building that you circumnavigate was 'home' until 1980 to 200 men living in cubicles only 6 foot square. One of the last relics of poverty and squalor for which the Grassmarket was at one time legendary, the building was completely renovated to provide accommodation and support to about a third of that number. It is now being converted again into flats and shops.

Turn right into the Grassmarket and then down the unsignposted **Aird's Close**, marked '83' above the door and '85' on the side of the pend. A short left turn and you double back to the Grassmarket once more by **Warden's Close**.

A plaque at the close mouth commemorates the spot where **Captain Porteous** was lynched by an Edinburgh mob on the night of 7th September, 1736. The crowd had started to stone the City Guard following the execution in the Grassmarket of a smuggler who had gained their sympathy by assisting his accomplice to escape. Captain Porteous,

Commander of the City Guard, ordered his men to fire, killing several bystanders. Tried and convicted of murder, Porteous was a prisoner in the Tolbooth when the rumour spread that he had been granted a Royal Pardon. The mob broke into the Tolbooth, seized Porteous, marched him to the Grassmarket and hanged him from a dyer's pole.

Turn right past Stan Wood's Fossils, the shop run by a fossil hunter whose finds are displayed in museums throughout the world.

Armorial doorway of Magdalen Chapel

Cross the foot of Candlemaker Row and go a few yards along the Cowgate to see the Magdalen Chapel, a charming little church behind its modest exterior. Unlike many churches in the city, it is often open to the public in the afternoons. The building is quite dwarfed by George IV Bridge which crosses the Cowgate at the level of the top of its steeple. Founded as an almshouse chapel by Michael MacQueen in 1537, it was managed by the Incorporation or Guild of Hammermen. One of the most venerable churches in the city, it preserves the oldest stained glass remaining in Scotland.

Carry on along the Cowgate under George IV Bridge. Take **Dyer's Close**, the first opening on the right. It runs along the side of the new Sheriff Court and was reinstated when the Courts were built. Turn right at the top of the close into Merchant Street, under another arch of George IV Bridge. Merchant Street is typical of the many contrasts of the Old Town, with pubs and clubs next to the prisoners' entrance to the Courts.

Turn left into Candlemaker Row and head up the hill. As its name suggests, Candlemaker Row was the home of the candlemaking industry. Because theirs was a very smelly and inflammable product, the candlemakers were required to locate their workshops away from the main centre of population. You can see the candlemakers' guild hall at the top of the street on the opposite side and before it a row of old houses of almost rural aspect.

At the top of Candlemaker Row stands the famous statue of Greyfriars Bobby.

Greyfriars Bobby was a small terrier who was so devoted to his master, John Gray, that when he died Bobby refused to leave his side. Gray was buried in the nearby churchyard and Bobby kept vigil at his master's grave—and at a nearby hostelry—for fourteen years until his death in 1872. The dog's loyalty to his master captured the imagination of the Victorians and the Queen herself took an interest in his welfare.

As well as this statue, dog lovers from as far away as the States have donated money to erect a memorial to Bobby in the churchyard and to put up a tombstone to his master. Bobby's story has inspired a film and several books, as well as the name of the adjoining pub.

Cross the top of Candlemaker Row and immediately opposite you will find the entrance to Greyfriars Churchyard. As well as containing a magnificent collection of sixteenth- to eighteenth-century tombs, the churchyard is a very pleasant place to linger, with some of the best views of Edinburgh Castle.

You cannot miss the tomb to Bobby in front of you as you enter. Take a sharp right to pass the memorial to his master on your left. At the end of the row of tombs, take the path which doubles back to the church. Go round to the west front and take the path off to your right. On your left you pass the grave of Walter Scott's parents just before an arch under the Flodden Wall and a splendid view of Heriot's Hospital.

Retrace your steps until you reach the first right turn. Take this and then turn right again to find the elaborate memorial to the Adam family, the last in the row. A plaster cast of some of its classical carvings is displayed beside it. On the left through an arch is the Covenanters' prison, where, it is claimed, 1,200 prisoners were confined in the open for five months after the Battle of Bothwell Bridge. Many prisoners inevitably died, some recanted and some 257 were eventually transported as slaves to the West Indies.

Turn left back towards the entrance with a fine row of monuments to Scotland's illustrious dead against the wall on your right. The tombs include the first Professor of Medicine at Edinburgh University and Patrick Miller, the amateur technologist who commissioned the design of the UK's first steam boat. Robert Burns joined him for its maiden voyage. Next door is the circular tomb of 'Bluidy Mackenzie', the hanging judge and founder of the Advocates' Library which in turn formed the core of the National Library of Scotland. His tomb is reputedly haunted. Turn left and right to regain the entrance to the churchyard.

Turn right and go along Forrest Road to the second set of traffic lights. Straight ahead is the tree-lined Middle Meadow Walk which leads down to the Meadows. This was formerly the Burgh Muir or common grazing lands for the citizens of Edinburgh and has been jealously protected as a green space ever since.

To the left of Middle Meadow Walk is the imposing, if soot-blackened, building of the University Medical School and on the right the Victorian pile of the Royal Infirmary. Built in the 1870s in Scots Baronial style to replace Adam's Infirmary (see Walk 9), the hospital has been extended many times. A new infirmary on the southern edge of the city is now being built to replace the present site.

Turn right at the traffic lights along Lauriston Place, passing immediately a fragment of the Telfer Wall. This was an extension of the Flodden Wall to take in the lands of Heriot's Hospital whose spacious grounds you now pass.

Heriot's Hospital was built in the early seventeenth century with money left in trust by George Heriot, a successful goldsmith, who had a shop at the north-east corner of St Giles. In 1597, Heriot was appointed goldsmith to Queen Anne of Denmark, the wife of James VI. As well as supplying jewellery, he lent money to the court and became very rich. His wealth and the coins that he carried on his person won him the nickname of 'Jingling Geordie'.

When James VI ascended to the throne of England in 1603, George followed him to London, and shared his good fortune. When he died there in 1623 he left provision in his will for a trust to found a home or hospital for the support of orphans of freemen of his native city.

The benefaction prospered, funding not only this grand hospital but also, in the nineteenth century, several elementary schools for poor children in the Old Town. It also supported the institution that was to become Heriot-Watt University.

Continue past the grounds of Heriot's Hospital to take first right into Heriot Place. Along its right side is a further stretch of the Telfer Wall. At the top of the **Vennel** the Telfer Wall meets the one remaining tower of the Flodden Wall. Take the steps down the Vennel. This was originally a steep, cobbled track running down the side of the Flodden Wall to the West Port, the gate which stood at its foot. The wall was breached in the early nineteenth century to create Brown's Place, the small square half-way down.

The left side of the Vennel lay outside the city walls in the separate burgh of Portsburgh. On your left as you descend is the shell of the former Portsburgh church, now awaiting a new use after many years as the dormitory of a Salvation Army Hostel.

At the foot of the Vennel, turn left and cross the West Port at the pedestrian crossing to take you back into the

The White Hart Inn, Grassmarket

Grassmarket. You will find a brief history of some of the area's more colourful events on the wall of the Fiddlers Arms. Cross over onto the 'island' on your right. Past the first row of parking bays there is a plaque celebrating 500 years of fairs in the Grassmarket, attached to a piece of the Castle rock. A fair is still held in the Grassmarket every summer, organised by the local community group.

Cross over and turn right along the north side of the Grassmarket, underneath the Castle. The recently opened Grannies' Green Steps climb up steeply past a former washing green to Johnston Terrace, by the side of the new Dance Base Studios. In the middle of the row of pubs and restaurants is the White Hart Inn, with its fine sign. Robert Burns and William Wordsworth stayed here when visiting the city. Look round the Grassmarket to appreciate the sheer diversity of building styles from seventeenth-century town houses to the Apex International Hotel, created from the 1960s concrete shell of part of Heriot-Watt University.

As you walk along the north side, you will see that one or two of the archways still retain their traditional close names. The sheer slope up to the Castle Rock means that there are only back courts behind. Turn left into **Castle Wynd South** and go up the steps. A steep, double right-angled climb takes you past a fragment of the original King's Wall and the Scottish Wildlife Trust's urban nature reserve on the left.

At the top of the steps, cross Johnston Terrace and take the dauntingly steep flight of steps, **Castle Wynd North**, immediately ahead. These lead you on to the Castle Esplanade and a well-earned view of the district that you have just explored.